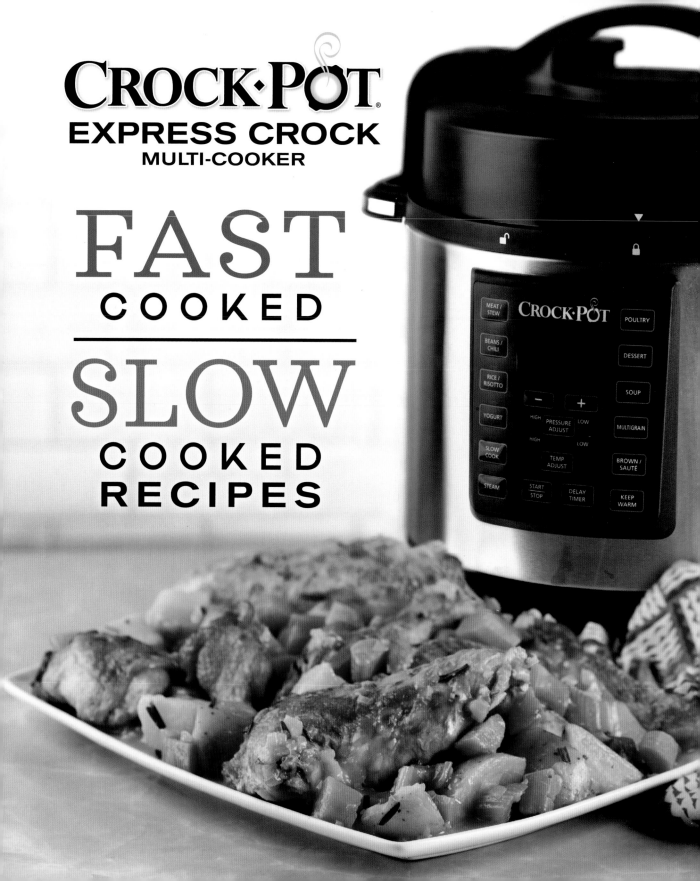

CROCK·POT®
EXPRESS CROCK
MULTI-COOKER

FAST
COOKED

SLOW
COOKED
RECIPES

Microwave Cooking: Microwave ovens vary in wattage. Use the cooking times as guidelines and check for doneness before adding more time.

Note: The recipes in this book are for use in the Crock-Pot® Express Crock Multi-Cooker. While today's multi-cookers are built with safety features, you MUST follow the instructions which come with your multi-cooker. IF YOU DO NOT FOLLOW THE SAFETY INSTRUCTIONS CAREFULLY, INJURY OR DAMAGE MAY RESULT.

TABLE OF CONTENTS

EXPRESS CROCK MULTI-COOKER 101

THE FAST PRESSURE COOKER WITH SLOW COOKER CONVENIENCE

In today's fast-paced world, you need a Multi-Cooker that can keep up with your lifestyle. Let the **CROCK-POT®** brand handle the pressure of mealtime with the **CROCK-POT®** Express Crock Multi-Cooker. Express Crock can cook meals up to 70% faster than traditional cooking, so you can spend less time in the kitchen and more time with your family.

When you're in a hurry, choose from 8 preset pressurized settings for the same slow-cooked taste you love in less time. Of course, if you're not ready to eat now, you can choose the SLOW COOK setting—just set the cook time and come back later to a delicious, hot dish that's ready to eat when you are.

Easily prepare any recipe in this cookbook—whether it's slow cooked, steamed, sautéed or pressure cooked—using one convenient appliance. The nonstick cooking pot resists stuck-on food and is dishwasher safe, making clean-up a breeze.

For more than 40 years, the **CROCK-POT®** brand has been your trusted brand for cooking convenience. The **CROCK-POT®** brand is a leader in one-pot cooking, and this Express Crock cooking collection is the perfect addition to your kitchen.

WHAT EXACTLY IS A PRESSURE COOKER?

It's a simple concept: Liquid is heated in a heavy pot with a lid that locks and forms an airtight seal. Since the steam from the hot liquid is trapped inside and can't evaporate, the pressure increases and raises the boiling point of the contents in the pot, and these items cook faster at a higher temperature. In general, pressure cooking can reduce cooking time to about one third of the time used in conventional cooking methods—and typically the time spent on pressure cooking is hands off. (There's no peeking or stirring when food is being cooked under pressure.)

EXPRESS CROCK COMPONENTS

Before beginning to cook, make sure you're familiar with the basic parts of the **CROCK-POT®** Express Crock Multi-Cooker. Always refer to your manual for more details and to answer questions about your specific model.

The **heating base** is where the electrical components are housed. It should never be immersed in water; to clean it, simply unplug the unit, wipe it with a damp cloth and dry it immediately.

The **cooking pot** holds the food and fits snugly into the heating base. It has a nonstick coating and is removable. Inside the cooking pot are markings to guide the fill level. The ⅓, ½ and ⅔ markings are handy guides to use in the recipes.

The **control panel** typically shows a time that indicates where the multi-cooker is in a particular function. The time counts down to zero from the number of minutes that were programmed. (When pressure cooking, the timing begins once the machine reaches pressure.)

The **steam release** valve is on top of the lid and is used to seal the pot or release steam. To seal the pot, move the valve to the sealing or locked position; to release pressure, move the valve to the venting or open position. This valve can pop off to clean, and to make sure nothing is blocking it.

The **bobber valve** controls the amount of pressure inside the pressure cooker and indicates when pressure cooking is taking place—the valve rises once the contents of the pot reach working pressure; it drops down when all the pressure has been released after cooking.

The **steam release valve cover** is a small stainless steel cage found on the inside of the lid that prevents the pressure cooker from clogging. It can be removed for cleaning.

The **gasket fixing ring** underneath the lid helps create a tight seal to facilitate pressure cooking. The sealing ring has a tendency to absorb strong odors from cooking (particularly from acidic ingredients); washing it regularly with warm soapy water will help these odors dissipate, as will storing your pressure cooker with the lid ring side up. If you cook both sweet and savory dishes frequently, you may want to purchase an extra sealing ring (so the scent of curry or pot roast doesn't affect your rice pudding or custard). Make sure to inspect the ring before cooking—if it has any splits or cracks, it will not work properly and should be replaced.

PRESSURE COOKING BASICS

Every recipe is slightly different, but most include these basic steps. Read through the entire recipe before beginning to cook so you'll know what ingredients to add and when to add them, which pressure cooking function to use, the cooking time and the release method.

1. BROWN/SAUTÉ: Many recipes call for sautéing vegetables or browning meat at the beginning of a recipe to add flavor. (Be sure to leave the lid off in this step.)

2. Add the ingredients as the recipe directs and secure the lid, making sure it is properly locked according to the instruction manual. Turn the pressure release valve to the "Seal" (closed) position.

3. Choose from the pressure cooking functions (STEAM, MEAT/STEW, BEANS/CHILI, RICE/RISOTTO, POULTRY, DESSERT, SOUP or MULTIGRAIN). Set pressure to HIGH or LOW and set the cooking time. Press START/STOP.

4. Once the pressure cooking is complete, use the pressure release method directed by the recipe. There are three types of releases:

Natural Pressure Release

Let the pressure slowly release on its own, which can take anywhere from 5 to 25 minutes (but is typically in the 10- to 15-minute range). The release time will be shorter for an Express Crock that is less full and longer for one that is more full. When the bobber valve lowers, the pressure is released and you can open the lid.

Quick Pressure Release

Use a towel or pot holder to manually turn the steam release valve to the venting or open position immediately after the cooking is complete. Be sure to get out of the way of the steam, and position the pressure cooker on your countertop so the steam doesn't get expelled straight into your cabinets (or in your face). It can take up to 2 minutes to fully release all the pressure.

Natural/Quick Pressure Combination Release

The recipe will instruct you to let the pressure release naturally for a certain amount of time (frequently for 10 minutes, and then do a quick release as directed.

RULES OF RELEASE

Releasing pressure can be a little confusing when you first start using an Express Crock. There's no need to worry at all about safety—you won't be able to open the lid until all the pressure has been released. And you don't need to guess which release to use since the recipes will tell you. But there are some important things to know about releasing pressure, especially when you start cooking and experimenting on your own.

Natural Pressure Release is best for meats (especially larger roasts and tough cuts), foods that generate a lot of foam, such as grains, dried beans and legumes, and foods that are primarily liquid, such as soups.

DONENESS TEMPERATURES

The best way to determine if meat is cooked properly is to test its internal temperature with an instant-read thermometer. To use an instant-read thermometer, insert it into the thickest part of the meat taking care not to poke it all the way through the meat and to avoid any bones. Leave the thermometer in the meat for about 20 seconds or until the needle stops moving. Instant-read thermometers are not heat-proof, so do not leave them in while cooking.

Beef, Lamb, or Veal

Ground Meat	165°F
Whole cuts	
Medium-Rare	145°F
Medium	160°F
Well-Done	170°F

Chicken, Turkey, or Other Poultry

Ground Chicken, Turkey, or Other Poultry	165°F
Boneless Chicken Breasts	165°F
Whole or Bone-in Chicken or Poultry; Breast Meat	170°F
Whole or Bone-in Chicken or Poultry; Dark Meat	180°F

Pork

Ground Pork	165°F
Ham, Purchased Fully Cooked	140°F
Ham, Purchased Uncooked	170°F
Whole cuts	
Medium	155°F
Well-Done	170°F

THE CONTROL PANEL

The cooking functions you'll find on the control panel are convenient shortcuts for some foods you may prepare regularly (rice, beans, stews, etc.) which use preset times and cooking levels. In this book we'll explore the basics of pressure cooking with recipes that use customized cooking times and pressure levels. So you'll be able to cook a wide variety of delicious dishes.

If you're accustomed to a stovetop pressure cooker, you'll need to make a few minor adjustments when using an electric one. Electric pressure cookers regulate heat automatically, so there's no worry about adjusting the heat on a burner to maintain pressure. Also, electric pressure cookers operate at less than the conventional pressure standard of 15 pounds per square inch (psi) used by stovetop pressure cookers. Most electric pressure cookers operate at 9 to 11 psi, which means that stovetop pressure cooker recipes can be adapted to electric models by adding a little more cooking time.

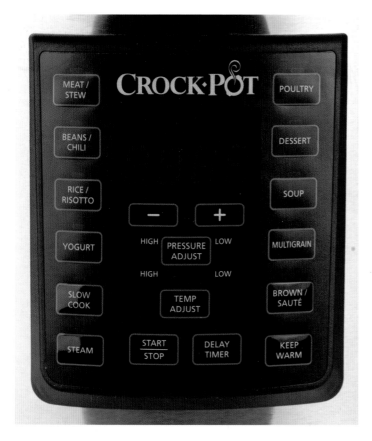

START/STOP

This button is used to start or stop a cooking program (such as when you are finished sautéing and are ready to start pressure cooking) or to turn off the pressure cooker. When the chosen time for pressure cooking is complete, the Express Crock will automatically switch to the Keep Warm program.

BROWN/SAUTÉ

This function can be used to brown meats or to sauté vegetables. Browning meats before pressure cooking or slow cooking helps seal in juices and can help keep the meat tender. Sautéing vegetables contributes to the flavor and color of the end dish.

KEEP WARM

This function is used to keep cooked food warm until you're ready to serve, or to reheat food that has been allowed to cool. When the chosen time for pressure cooking is complete, the Express Crock will automatically switch to the KEEP WARM program.

SLOW COOK

The SLOW COOK function does not use pressure in the cooking process, but some pressure can build inside the unit during cooking. When using this function, ensure the Steam Release Valve is in the "Release" position. This function will cook similarly to standard slow cookers, using lower temperatures and longer cooking times.

STEAM

This function is perfect for gently steaming fish and vegetables. When steaming, use the steaming rack. The maximum capacity of liquid should be just under the rack wires, so that the liquid is not touching the food.

COOKING FUNCTION	DEFAULT SETTING	PRESSURE ADJUSTMENTS	TEMPERATURE ADJUSTMENTS	COOK TIME RANGE
MEAT/STEW	HIGH pressure/ 35 minutes	LOW-HIGH	N/A	15 minutes– 2 hours
BEANS/CHILI	HIGH pressure/ 20 minutes	LOW-HIGH	N/A	5 minutes– 2 hours
RICE/RISOTTO	LOW pressure/ 12 minutes	LOW-HIGH	N/A	6 minutes– 30 minutes
YOGURT	LOW temp/ 8 hours	N/A	LOW-HIGH	LOW: 6 hours– 12 hours HIGH: N/A
SLOW COOK	HIGH temp/ 4 hours	N/A	LOW-HIGH	30 minutes– 20 hours
STEAM	HIGH pressure/ 10 minutes	LOW-HIGH	N/A	3 minutes– 1 hour
POULTRY	HIGH pressure/ 15 minutes	LOW-HIGH	N/A	15 minutes– 2 hours
DESSERT	LOW pressure/ 10 minutes	LOW-HIGH	N/A	5 minutes– 2 hours
SOUP	HIGH pressure/ 30 minutes	LOW-HIGH	N/A	5 minutes– 2 hours
MULTIGRAIN	HIGH pressure/ 40 minutes	LOW-HIGH	N/A	10 minutes– 2 hours
BROWN/SAUTÉ	HIGH temp/ 30 minutes	N/A	LOW-HIGH	5 minutes– 30 minutes
KEEP WARM	Warm temp/ 4 hours	N/A	WARM	30 minutes– 4 hours

POT ROAST WITH
BACON AND MUSHROOMS
(page 116)

TIPS, TRICKS, DOS AND DON'TS

- Read the manual before beginning. There may be features you won't use, but it can help you understand how the machine works—and see all its possibilities.

- Don't overfill the Express Crock—the total amount of food and liquid should not exceed the maximum level marked on the inner cooking pot. Generally it is best not to fill the cooking pot more than two thirds full. When cooking foods that expand during cooking such as beans and grains, do not fill it more than half full.

- You do not need too many additional products when using the Express Crock, but a few simple kitchen items are useful for certain recipes. Heatproof containers such as soufflé dishes, baking dishes, ramekins or custard cups are often used to cook desserts that contain a lot of liquid, such as bread puddings or custards. They may be made of ceramic, metal, silicone or heatproof glass and should always be used with the steaming rack. In addition, foil handles (see diagram page 13) are recommended when using these containers to make lifting them from the Express Crock easier.

- Make sure there is always some liquid in the Express Crock before cooking because a minimum amount (usually 1 cup) is required to come up to pressure. (However, if the recipe contains a large amount of vegetables, you may be able to use a bit less since the vegetables will create their own liquid.)

- Always check that the pressure release valve is in the right position before you start pressure cooking. The food simply won't get cooked if the valve is not in the sealing or locked position because there will not be enough pressure in the Express Crock.

- Never try to force the lid open after cooking—if the lid won't open, that means the pressure has not fully released. (As a safety feature, the lid remains locked until the float valve drops down.)

- Save the thickeners for after the pressure or slow cooking is done. These recipes often end up with a lot of flavorful liquid left in the Express Crock when cooking is complete. Flour or cornstarch mixtures can thicken these liquids into delicious sauces. Use the BROWN/SAUTÉ function while incorporating the thickeners into the cooking liquid, and then cook and stir until the desired consistency is reached.

- Keep in mind that cooking times in some recipes may vary. These are approximate times and numerous variables may cause your results to be different. For example, the freshness of dried beans affects their cooking time (older beans take longer to cook), as does what they are cooked with— hard water (water that is high in mineral content), acidic ingredients,

FAST-COOKED
SUCCOTASH
(page 156)

sugar and salt levels can also affect cooking times. So be flexible and experiment with what works best for you—you can always check the doneness of your food and add more time.

- Set reasonable expectations, i.e., don't expect everything you cook in the **CROCK-POT®** Express Crock Multi-Cooker to be ready in a few minutes. Even though pressure cooking reduces many conventional cooking times dramatically, nothing is literally "fast"—it will always take time to get up to pressure, and then to release it. You can make fabulous pot roast, irresistible pulled pork, hearty soups, stews, chilies and risottos in a fraction of the time they might take on the stove. But if you're looking for casseroles with crispy toppings, charred meats and vegetables, or side dishes with crunch, then this is not the right machine for the job. Use the **CROCK-POT®** Express Crock Multi-Cooker for the types of recipes that work best, and then enjoy the time saved—and all the delicious results! The possibilities are endless!

FOIL HANDLES: To easily lift a dish or a meat loaf from a **CROCK-POT®** Express Crock Multi-Cooker, make foil handles as shown below.

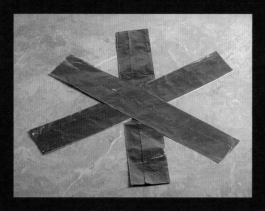

1. Tear off three 18×2-inch strips of heavy-duty foil. Crisscross the strips so they resemble the spokes of a wheel. Place the dish of food in the center of the strips.

2. Pull the strips up and over the dish or food; using the foil handles, lift the dish or food and place it into the **CROCK-POT®** Express Crock Multi-Cooker. Leave the strips in during cooking so you can easily lift the item out again when it's ready.

CHAPTER 1

APPETIZERS

CHICKEN PÂTÉ
(page 44)

PULLED PORK SLIDERS
(page 40)

BARLEY "CAVIAR"
(page 26)

ASIAN LETTUCE WRAPS
(page 32)

CHIPOTLE TURKEY
SLOPPY JOE SLIDERS
(page 20)

THAI COCONUT
CHICKEN MEATBALLS
(page 34)

RASPBERRY-BALSAMIC
GLAZED MEATBALLS (PRESSURE)

MAKES ABOUT 16 SERVINGS

- 1 bag (2 pounds) frozen fully cooked meatballs
- 1 cup raspberry preserves
- 3 tablespoons sugar

- 3 tablespoons balsamic vinegar
- 1 tablespoon plus 1½ teaspoons Worcestershire sauce

- ¼ teaspoon red pepper flakes
- 1 tablespoon grated fresh ginger

1 Coat inside of **CROCK-POT®** Express Crock Multi-Cooker with nonstick cooking spray. Add frozen meatballs.

2 Combine preserves, sugar, vinegar, Worcestershire sauce and red pepper flakes in small bowl. Reserve ½ cup glaze in refrigerator. Pour remaining glaze mixture over meatballs in Express Crock; toss to coat. Secure lid. Press BEANS/CHILI, set pressure to HIGH and time to 8 minutes. Make sure Steam Release Valve is in the "Seal" (closed) position. Press START/STOP.

3 Once cooking is complete, quick release pressure. Remove meatballs to large bowl. Press BROWN/ SAUTÉ on Express Crock; stir reserved glaze and ginger into cooking liquid. Cook, uncovered, on HIGH 5 minutes or until thickened slightly, stirring occasionally. Add meatballs; toss to coat.

RASPBERRY-BALSAMIC
GLAZED MEATBALLS (SLOW COOK)

MAKES ABOUT 16 SERVINGS

- 1 bag (2 pounds) frozen fully cooked meatballs
- 1 cup raspberry preserves
- 3 tablespoons sugar

- 3 tablespoons balsamic vinegar
- 1 tablespoon plus 1½ teaspoons Worcestershire sauce

- ¼ teaspoon red pepper flakes
- 1 tablespoon grated fresh ginger

1 Coat inside of **CROCK-POT®** Express Crock Multi-Cooker with nonstick cooking spray. Add frozen meatballs.

2 Combine preserves, sugar, vinegar, Worcestershire sauce and red pepper flakes in small microwavable bowl. Microwave on HIGH 45 seconds; stir. Microwave 15 seconds or until melted. Reserve ½ cup glaze in refrigerator. Pour remaining glaze mixture over meatballs in Express Crock; stir until well coated. Secure lid. Press SLOW COOK, set temperature to LOW and time to 5 hours. Make sure Steam Release Valve is in the "Release" (open) position. Press START/STOP.

3 Once cooking is complete, press BROWN/SAUTÉ on Express Crock. Stir in reserved glaze and ginger. Cook, uncovered, on HIGH 5 to 10 minutes or until thickened slightly, stirring occasionally.

ANGELIC DEVILED EGGS (PRESSURE)

6 eggs

¼ cup cottage cheese

3 tablespoons ranch dressing

2 teaspoons Dijon mustard

2 tablespoons minced fresh chives or dill

1 tablespoon diced well-drained pimientos or roasted red pepper

1 Place 1½ cups water and steaming rack in bottom of **CROCK-POT®** Express Crock Multi-Cooker. Place eggs on rack. Secure lid. Press STEAM, set pressure to LOW and time to 10 minutes. Make sure Steam Release Valve is in the "Seal" (closed) position. Press START/STOP.

2 Once cooking is complete, quick release pressure. Remove eggs to large bowl of ice water; let cool 5 to 10 minutes.

3 Peel eggs; cut in half lengthwise. Remove yolks, reserving 3 yolk halves. Discard remaining yolks or reserve for another use. Place egg whites, cut sides up, on serving plate; cover with plastic wrap. Refrigerate while preparing filling. Combine cottage cheese, dressing, mustard and reserved yolk halves in small bowl; mash with fork until well blended. Stir in chives and pimientos. Spoon cottage cheese mixture into egg whites. Cover; refrigerate at least 1 hour before serving.

ANGELIC DEVILED EGGS (SLOW COOK)

6 eggs

¼ cup cottage cheese

3 tablespoons ranch dressing

2 teaspoons Dijon mustard

2 tablespoons minced fresh chives or dill

1 tablespoon diced well-drained pimientos or roasted red pepper

1 Place 1½ cups water and rack in bottom of **CROCK-POT®** Express Crock Multi-Cooker. Place eggs on rack. Secure lid. Press SLOW COOK, set temperature to LOW and time to 3½ hours. Make sure Steam Release Valve is in the "Release" (open) position. Press START/STOP.

2 Once cooking is complete, remove eggs to large bowl of ice water. Let cool 5 to 10 minutes.

3 Peel eggs; cut in half lengthwise. Remove yolks, reserving 3 yolk halves. Discard remaining yolks or reserve for another use. Place egg whites, cut sides up, on serving plate; cover with plastic wrap. Refrigerate while preparing filling. Combine cottage cheese, dressing, mustard and reserved yolk halves in small bowl; mash with fork until well blended. Stir in chives and pimientos. Spoon cottage cheese mixture into egg whites. Cover; refrigerate at least 1 hour before serving.

TIPS: You can use this method to cook 3 to 12 eggs. If you don't need to use the eggs right away, store them unpeeled in the refrigerator for up to 1 week.

CHIPOTLE TURKEY
SLOPPY JOE SLIDERS (PRESSURE)

1 pound turkey Italian sausage links, casings removed

1 package (14 ounces) frozen green and red bell pepper strips with onions

1 cup chicken broth

1 can (6 ounces) tomato paste

1 tablespoon quick-cooking tapioca

1 tablespoon minced canned chipotle peppers in adobo sauce, plus 1 tablespoon sauce

2 teaspoons ground cumin

½ teaspoon dried thyme

12 corn muffins or small dinner rolls, split and toasted

1 Press BROWN/SAUTÉ on **CROCK-POT**® Express Crock Multi-Cooker. Add sausage; cook, uncovered, on HIGH 6 to 8 minutes, stirring to break up meat. Drain fat.

2 Add pepper strips with onions, broth, tomato paste, tapioca, chipotle peppers with sauce, cumin and thyme; stir to blend. Secure lid. Press POULTRY, set pressure to HIGH and time to 15 minutes. Make sure Steam Release Valve is in the "Seal" (closed) position. Press START/STOP.

3 Once cooking is complete, quick release pressure. Serve on corn muffins.

CHIPOTLE TURKEY
SLOPPY JOE SLIDERS (SLOW COOK)

MAKES 12 SLIDERS

1 pound turkey Italian sausage links, casings removed

1 package (14 ounces) frozen green and red bell pepper strips with onions

1 can (6 ounces) tomato paste

1 tablespoon quick-cooking tapioca

1 tablespoon minced canned chipotle peppers in adobo sauce, plus 1 tablespoon sauce

2 teaspoons ground cumin

½ teaspoon dried thyme

12 corn muffins or small dinner rolls, split and toasted

1 Press BROWN/SAUTÉ on **CROCK-POT**® Express Crock Multi-Cooker. Add sausage; cook, uncovered, 5 to 7 minutes or until browned, stirring to break up meat. Drain fat.

2 Stir in pepper strips with onions, tomato paste, tapioca, chipotle peppers with sauce, cumin and thyme. Secure lid. Press SLOW COOK, set temperature to LOW and time to 8 hours. Make sure Steam Release Valve is in the "Release" (open) position. Press START/STOP.

3 Once cooking is complete, serve on corn muffins.

BEANS AND SPINACH BRUSCHETTA
(PRESSURE)

1 cup cannellini beans, rinsed and sorted

2 cups vegetable broth

3 cloves garlic, minced

Salt and black pepper

6 cups spinach, loosely packed and finely chopped

1 tablespoon red wine vinegar

16 slices whole grain baguette, toasted

1 Combine beans, broth, garlic, salt and pepper in **CROCK-POT®** Express Crock Multi-Cooker. Secure lid. Press BEANS/CHILI, set pressure to HIGH and time to 35 minutes. Make sure Steam Release Valve is in the "Seal" (closed) position. Press START/STOP.

2 Once cooking is complete, natural release 10 minutes. Release remaining pressure. Drain beans, reserving broth. Place beans and ¼ cup reserved broth in food processor or blender; blend 3 to 4 minutes or until desired consistency, adding additional reserved broth if necessary.

3 Add spinach, 1 cup reserved broth and vinegar to Express Crock. Secure lid. Press STEAM, set pressure to LOW and time to 3 minutes. Once cooking is completely, quick release pressure. Top baguettes with bean mixture and spinach.

BEANS AND SPINACH BRUSCHETTA
(SLOW COOK)

2 cans (about 15 ounces *each*) cannellini beans, rinsed and drained

3 cloves garlic, minced

Salt and black pepper

6 cups spinach, loosely packed and finely chopped

1 tablespoon red wine vinegar

16 slices whole grain baguette, toasted

1 Combine beans, garlic, salt and pepper in **CROCK-POT®** Express Crock Multi-Cooker; stir to blend. Secure lid. Press SLOW COOK, set temperature to LOW and time to 3 hours. Make sure Steam Release Valve is in the "Release" (open) position. Press START/STOP.

2 Once cooking is complete and beans are tender, drain beans and reserve broth. Place beans and ¼ cup reserved broth in food processor or blender; blend 3 to 4 minutes or until desired consistency, adding additional reserved broth if necessary. Combine any remaining broth, spinach and vinegar in large bowl; stir to blend. Top baguettes with bean mixture and spinach.

HONEY-GLAZED
CHICKEN WINGS (PRESSURE)

MAKES 6 SERVINGS

- 3 tablespoons vegetable oil, divided
- 3 pounds chicken wings
- 1 cup honey
- ¼ cup soy sauce
- 2 tablespoons tomato paste
- 2 teaspoons water
- 1 clove garlic, minced
- 1 teaspoon sugar
- 1 teaspoon black pepper

1 Press BROWN/SAUTÉ on **CROCK-POT®** Express Crock Multi-Cooker; heat 1½ tablespoons oil on HIGH. Add wings in batches; cook, uncovered, 2 to 3 minutes on each side or until browned. Remove to large paper towel-lined plate.

2 Combine remaining 1½ tablespoons oil, honey, soy sauce, tomato paste, water, garlic, sugar and pepper in Express Crock; stir to blend. Add wings; turn to coat. Secure lid. Press POULTRY, set pressure to HIGH and time to 15 minutes. Make sure Steam Release Valve is in the "Seal" (closed) position. Press START/STOP.

3 Once cooking is complete, quick release pressure. Remove wings to large serving plate. Press BROWN/SAUTÉ on Express Crock; cook sauce, uncovered, on HIGH 5 minutes or until thickened. Serve wings with sauce.

HONEY-GLAZED
CHICKEN WINGS (SLOW COOK)

MAKES 6 SERVINGS

- 3 tablespoons vegetable oil, divided
- 3 pounds chicken wings
- 1 cup honey
- ½ cup soy sauce
- 2 tablespoons tomato paste
- 2 teaspoons water
- 1 clove garlic, minced
- 1 teaspoon sugar
- 1 teaspoon black pepper

1 Press BROWN/SAUTÉ on **CROCK-POT®** Express Crock Multi-Cooker; heat 1½ tablespoons oil on HIGH. Add wings in batches; cook, uncovered, 1 to 2 minutes on each side or until browned. Press START/STOP.

2 Combine remaining 1½ tablespoons oil, honey, soy sauce, tomato paste, water, garlic, sugar and pepper in medium bowl; stir to blend. Pour sauce over wings. Secure lid. Press SLOW COOK, set temperature and time to LOW 6 to 8 hours or to HIGH 3 to 4 hours. Make sure Steam Release Valve is in the "Release" (open) position. Press START/STOP.

3 Once cooking is complete, remove wings to large serving platter. Press BROWN/SAUTÉ on Express Crock; cook sauce, uncovered, on HIGH 5 to 10 minutes or until thickened. Serve wings with sauce.

BARLEY "CAVIAR" (PRESSURE)

MAKES 8 APPETIZERS

1½ cups vegetable broth

¾ cup uncooked pearl barley

1 teaspoon salt, divided

2 tablespoons plus 1 teaspoon olive oil

4 teaspoons white wine vinegar

¼ teaspoon ground cumin

⅛ teaspoon black pepper

½ cup sliced pimiento-stuffed olives

½ cup finely chopped red bell pepper

1 stalk celery, chopped

1 large shallot, finely chopped

1 jalapeño pepper,* minced, or ¼ teaspoon red pepper flakes

8 leaves endive or Bibb lettuce

*Jalapeño peppers can sting and irritate the skin, so wear rubber gloves when handling peppers and do not touch your eyes.

1 Add broth, barley and ½ teaspoon salt to **CROCK-POT®** Express Crock Multi-Cooker. Secure lid. Press MULTIGRAIN, set pressure to HIGH and time to 22 minutes. Make sure Steam Release Valve is in the "Seal" (closed) position. Press START/STOP.

2 Meanwhile, combine oil, vinegar, remaining ½ teaspoon salt, cumin and black pepper in small bowl; stir to blend.

3 Once cooking is complete, quick release pressure. Stir in olives, bell pepper, celery, shallot and jalapeño pepper. Pour oil mixture over barley mixture in Express Crock; stir gently to coat. Let stand 10 minutes. To serve, spoon barley mixture evenly into endive leaves.

BARLEY "CAVIAR" (SLOW COOK)

MAKES 8 APPETIZERS

4½ cups vegetable broth

¾ cup uncooked pearl barley

1 teaspoon salt, divided

2 tablespoons plus 1 teaspoon olive oil

4 teaspoons white wine vinegar

¼ teaspoon ground cumin

⅛ teaspoon black pepper

½ cup sliced pimiento-stuffed olives

½ cup finely chopped red bell pepper

1 stalk celery, chopped

1 large shallot, finely chopped

1 jalapeño pepper,* minced, or ¼ teaspoon red pepper flakes

8 leaves endive or Bibb lettuce

*Jalapeño peppers can sting and irritate the skin, so wear rubber gloves when handling peppers and do not touch your eyes.

1 Add broth, barley and ½ teaspoon salt to **CROCK-POT®** Express Crock Multi-Cooker. Secure lid. Press SLOW COOK, set temperature and time to LOW 4 to 5 hours or to HIGH 2½ to 3 hours. Make sure Steam Release Valve is in the "Release" (open) position. Press START/STOP.

2   Meanwhile, combine oil, vinegar, remaining ½ teaspoon salt, cumin and black pepper in small bowl; stir to blend.

3   Once cooking is complete, barley is tender and liquid is absorbed; stir in olives, bell pepper, celery, shallot and jalapeño pepper. Pour oil mixture over barley mixture in Express Crock; stir gently to coat. Let stand 10 minutes. To serve, spoon barley mixture evenly into endive leaves.

CARNITAS TACOS (PRESSURE)

MAKES 12 SERVINGS

1½ pounds boneless pork loin

1 onion, chopped

1 cup chicken broth

1 tablespoon chili powder

2 teaspoons ground cumin

1 teaspoon dried oregano

½ teaspoon minced canned chipotle peppers in adobo sauce

½ cup pico de gallo

2 tablespoons chopped fresh cilantro

½ teaspoon salt

12 (6-inch) corn tortillas

¾ cup (3 ounces) shredded sharp Cheddar cheese

3 tablespoons sour cream

1 Combine pork, onion, broth, chili powder, cumin, oregano and chipotle peppers in **CROCK-POT®** Express Crock Multi-Cooker. Secure lid. Press MEAT/STEW, set pressure to HIGH and timing to 35 minutes. Make sure Steam Release Valve is in the "Seal" (closed) position. Press START/STOP.

2 Once cooking is complete, natural release pressure 10 minutes. Release remaining pressure. Remove pork to large cutting board; shred with two forks.

3 Press BROWN/SAUTÉ on Express Crock; cook sauce, uncovered, on HIGH 10 minutes or until thickened. Return pork to Express Crock. Stir in pico de gallo, cilantro and salt. Cut three circles from each tortilla with 2-inch biscuit cutter. Top each evenly with pork, cheese and sour cream.

CARNITAS TACOS (SLOW COOK)

MAKES 12 SERVINGS

1½ pounds boneless pork loin

1 onion, finely chopped

½ cup chicken broth

1 tablespoon chili powder

2 teaspoons ground cumin

1 teaspoon dried oregano

½ teaspoon minced canned chipotle peppers in adobo sauce

½ cup pico de gallo

2 tablespoons chopped fresh cilantro

½ teaspoon salt

12 (6-inch) corn tortillas

¾ cup (3 ounces) shredded sharp Cheddar cheese

3 tablespoons sour cream

1 Combine pork, onion, broth, chili powder, cumin, oregano and chipotle peppers in **CROCK-POT®** Express Crock Multi-Cooker; stir to blend. Secure lid. Press SLOW COOK, set temperature and time to LOW 6 hours or HIGH 3 hours. Make sure Steam Release Valve is in the "Release" (open) position. Press START/STOP.

2 Once cooking is complete, remove pork to large cutting board; shred with two forks.

3 Press BROWN/SAUTÉ on Express Crock; cook sauce, uncovered, on HIGH 10 minutes or until thickened. Return pork to Express Crock. Stir in pico de gallo, cilantro and salt. Cut three circles from each tortilla with 2-inch biscuit cutter. Top each evenly with pork, cheese and sour cream.

CAPONATA (PRESSURE)

2 tablespoons vegetable oil

1 medium onion, chopped

1 medium eggplant (about 1 pound), peeled and cut into ½-inch pieces

1 medium tomato, cut into ½-inch pieces

1 red bell pepper, cut into ½-inch pieces

½ cup medium salsa

2 tablespoons capers, drained

2 tablespoons balsamic vinegar

3 cloves garlic, minced

1 teaspoon dried oregano

⅓ cup packed fresh basil, cut into thin strips

2 loaves (24 slices) Italian or French bread, sliced and toasted

1 Press BROWN/SAUTÉ on **CROCK-POT®** Express Crock Multi-Cooker; heat oil on HIGH. Add onion; cook and stir 3 minutes or until softened. Add eggplant, tomato, bell pepper, salsa, capers, vinegar, garlic and oregano; stir to blend. Secure lid. Press STEAM, set pressure to LOW and time to 3 minutes. Make sure Steam Release Valve is in the "Seal" (closed) position. Press START/STOP.

2 Once cooking is complete, quick release pressure. Stir in basil; serve on bread.

CAPONATA (SLOW COOK)

1 medium eggplant (about 1 pound), peeled and cut into ½-inch pieces

1 can (about 14 ounces) diced tomatoes

1 medium onion, chopped

1 red bell pepper, cut into ½-inch pieces

½ cup mild salsa

¼ cup extra virgin olive oil

2 tablespoons capers, drained

2 tablespoons balsamic vinegar

3 cloves garlic, minced

1 teaspoon dried oregano

⅓ cup packed fresh basil, cut into thin strips

2 loaves (24 slices) Italian or French bread, sliced and toasted

1 Combine eggplant, tomatoes, onion, bell pepper, salsa, oil, capers, vinegar, garlic and oregano in **CROCK-POT®** Express Crock Multi-Cooker; stir to blend. Secure lid. Press SLOW COOK, set temperature to LOW and time to 7 hours. Make sure Steam Release Valve is in the "Release" (open) position. Press START/STOP.

2 Once cooking is complete, stir in basil and serve on bread.

ASIAN LETTUCE WRAPS (PRESSURE)

2 teaspoons canola oil

1½ pounds boneless, skinless chicken breasts, chopped into ¼-inch pieces

2 leeks, trimmed and chopped into ¼-inch pieces

1 cup shiitake mushrooms, stems removed and caps chopped into ¼-inch pieces

1 stalk celery, chopped into ¼-inch pieces

1 tablespoon oyster sauce

1 tablespoon soy sauce

1 teaspoon dark sesame oil

¼ teaspoon black pepper

½ pound large raw shrimp, peeled, deveined and cut into ¼-inch pieces

1 bag (8 ounces) coleslaw or broccoli slaw mix

½ red bell pepper, cut into thin strips

3 tablespoons unsalted dry roasted peanuts, coarsely chopped

Hoisin sauce

12 crisp romaine lettuce leaves, white ribs removed and patted dry

Fresh whole chives

1 Press BROWN/SAUTÉ on **CROCK-POT®** Express Crock Multi-Cooker; heat canola oil on HIGH. Add chicken; cook, uncovered, 5 minutes or until browned on all sides. Add leeks, mushrooms, celery, oyster sauce, soy sauce, sesame oil and black pepper; stir to blend. Secure lid. Press BEANS/CHILI, set pressure to HIGH and time to 5 minutes. Make sure Steam Release Valve is in the "Seal" (closed) position. Press START/STOP.

2 Once cooking is complete, natural release pressure 10 minutes. Release remaining pressure. Press BROWN/SAUTÉ on Express Crock. Stir in shrimp, slaw mix and bell pepper; cook, uncovered, on HIGH 3 to 5 minutes or until shrimp are pink and opaque. Remove mixture to large bowl; stir in peanuts.

3 To serve, spread hoisin sauce on lettuce leaves. Add meat mixture and tightly roll. Secure by tying chives around rolled leaves.

ASIAN LETTUCE WRAPS (SLOW COOK)

2 teaspoons canola oil

1½ pounds boneless, skinless chicken breasts, chopped into ¼-inch pieces

2 leeks, trimmed and chopped into ¼-inch pieces

1 cup shiitake mushrooms, stems removed and caps chopped into ¼-inch pieces

1 stalk celery, chopped into ¼-inch pieces

1 tablespoon oyster sauce

1 tablespoon soy sauce

1 teaspoon dark sesame oil

¼ teaspoon black pepper

2 tablespoons water

1 bag (8 ounces) coleslaw or broccoli slaw mix

½ red bell pepper, cut into thin strips

½ pound large raw shrimp, peeled, deveined and cut into ¼-inch pieces

3 tablespoons dry roasted peanuts, coarsely chopped

Hoisin sauce

12 crisp romaine lettuce leaves, white ribs removed and patted dry

Fresh whole chives

1 Press BROWN/SAUTÉ on **CROCK-POT®** Express Crock Multi-Cooker; heat canola oil on HIGH. Add chicken; cook, uncovered, 5 minutes or until browned on all sides. Add leeks, mushrooms, celery, oyster sauce, soy sauce, sesame oil, black pepper and water in Express Crock. Toss slaw and bell pepper in medium bowl; place in single layer on top of chicken mixture.

2 Secure lid. Press SLOW COOK, set temperature and time to LOW 4 to 5 hours or to HIGH 2 to 2½ hours. Make sure Steam Release Valve is in the "Release" (open) position. Press START/STOP. Stir in shrimp during last 20 minutes of cooking.

3 Once cooking is complete, chicken is cooked through and shrimp are pink and opaque; stir in peanuts. To serve, spread hoisin sauce on lettuce leaves. Add meat mixture and tightly roll. Secure by tying chives around rolled leaves.

THAI COCONUT
CHICKEN MEATBALLS (PRESSURE)

1 pound ground chicken

2 green onions, chopped

1 clove garlic, minced

2 teaspoons toasted sesame oil

2 teaspoons mirin

1 teaspoon fish sauce

1 cup chicken broth

½ cup unsweetened canned coconut milk

2 teaspoons packed brown sugar

2 teaspoons Thai red curry paste

1 tablespoon canola oil

2 teaspoons lime juice

2 tablespoons water

1 tablespoon cornstarch

1 Combine chicken, green onions, garlic, sesame oil, mirin and fish sauce in large bowl; mix well. Shape chicken mixture into 1½-inch meatballs. Combine broth, coconut milk, brown sugar and curry paste in small bowl; stir to blend. Reserve half of sauce.

2 Press BROWN/SAUTÉ on **CROCK-POT®** Express Crock Multi-Cooker; heat canola oil on HIGH. Add meatballs in batches; cook, uncovered, 5 to 8 minutes or until browned. Add half of coconut milk mixture and meatballs back into to Express Crock. Secure lid. Press BEANS/CHILI, set pressure to HIGH and time to 8 minutes. Make sure Steam Release Valve is in the "Seal" (closed) position. Press START/STOP.

3 Once cooking is complete, quick release pressure. Remove meatballs to large bowl with reserved sauce. Press BROWN/SAUTÉ on Express Crock. Stir lime juice into cooking liquid. Stir water into cornstarch in small bowl until smooth; whisk into cooking liquid. Cook, uncovered, on HIGH 5 minutes or until thickened. Add meatballs; toss to coat.

THAI COCONUT
CHICKEN MEATBALLS (SLOW COOK)

1 pound ground chicken

2 green onions, chopped

1 clove garlic, minced

2 teaspoons toasted sesame oil

2 teaspoons mirin

1 teaspoon fish sauce

½ cup unsweetened canned coconut milk

¼ cup chicken broth

2 teaspoons packed brown sugar

1 teaspoon Thai red curry paste

1 tablespoon canola oil

2 teaspoons lime juice

2 tablespoons water

1 tablespoon cornstarch

1 Combine chicken, green onions, garlic, sesame oil, mirin and fish sauce in large bowl; mix well. Shape mixture into 1½-inch meatballs. Combine coconut milk, broth, brown sugar and curry paste in small bowl; stir to blend. Reserve half of sauce.

2   Press BROWN/SAUTÉ on **CROCK-POT®** Express Crock Multi-Cooker; heat canola oil on HIGH. Add meatballs in batches; cook, uncovered, 5 to 8 minutes or until browned on all sides. Add half of coconut milk mixture. Secure lid. Press SLOW COOK, set temperature to HIGH and time to 3½ to 4 hours. Make sure Steam Release Valve is in the "Release" (open) position. Press START/STOP.

3   Once cooking is complete, remove meatballs to large bowl with reserved sauce. Press BROWN/SAUTÉ on Express Crock. Stir lime juice into cooking liquid. Stir water into cornstarch in small bowl until smooth; whisk into cooking liquid. Cook, uncovered, on HIGH 5 minutes or until sauce is slightly thickened. Add meatballs; toss to coat.

WARM MOROCCAN-STYLE
BEAN DIP (PRESSURE)

2 teaspoons canola oil

1 small onion, chopped

2 cloves garlic, minced

2 cans (about 15 ounces *each*) cannellini beans, rinsed and drained

¾ cup canned diced tomatoes

½ cup vegetable broth

1 teaspoon salt

½ teaspoon ground turmeric

¼ teaspoon ground cumin

¼ teaspoon ground cinnamon

¼ teaspoon paprika

¼ teaspoon black pepper

⅛ teaspoon ground cloves

⅛ teaspoon ground red pepper

2 tablespoons plain yogurt

1 tablespoon cold water

¼ teaspoon dried mint (optional)

Warm pita bread rounds, cut into wedges

1 Press BROWN/SAUTÉ on **CROCK-POT®** Express Crock Multi-Cooker; heat oil on HIGH. Add onion; cook and stir, uncovered, 3 minutes or until translucent. Add garlic; cook and stir 30 seconds. Stir in beans, tomatoes, broth, salt, turmeric, cumin, cinnamon, paprika, black pepper, cloves and ground red pepper. Secure lid. Press BEANS/CHILI, set pressure to HIGH and time to 10 minutes. Make sure Steam Release Valve is in the "Seal" (closed) position. Press START/STOP.

2 Once cooking is complete, natural release pressure 10 minutes. Release remaining pressure. Remove bean mixture and enough cooking liquid to food processor or blender; process using on/off pulsing action until coarsely chopped. Remove to large serving bowl.

3 Beat yogurt and cold water in small bowl until well combined. Drizzle over bean dip. Garnish with mint. Serve warm with pita bread.

WARM MOROCCAN-STYLE
BEAN DIP (SLOW COOK)

2 teaspoons canola oil

1 small onion, chopped

2 cloves garlic, minced

2 cans (about 15 ounces *each*) cannellini beans, rinsed and drained

¾ cup canned diced tomatoes

1 teaspoon salt

½ teaspoon ground turmeric

¼ teaspoon ground cumin

¼ teaspoon ground cinnamon

¼ teaspoon paprika

¼ teaspoon black pepper

⅛ teaspoon ground cloves

⅛ teaspoon ground red pepper

2 tablespoons plain yogurt

1 tablespoon cold water

¼ teaspoon dried mint (optional)

Warm pita bread rounds, cut into wedges

1. Press BROWN/SAUTÉ on **CROCK-POT®** Express Crock Multi-Cooker; heat oil on HIGH. Add onion; cook and stir, uncovered, 3 minutes or until translucent. Add garlic; cook and stir 30 seconds. Stir in beans, tomatoes, salt, turmeric, cumin, cinnamon, paprika, black pepper, cloves and ground red pepper. Secure lid. Press SLOW COOK, set temperature to LOW and time to 6 hours. Make sure Steam Release Valve is in the "Release" (open) position. Press START/STOP.

2. Once cooking is complete, remove bean mixture and enough cooking liquid to food processor or blender. Process using on/off pulsing action until coarsely chopped. Remove to large serving bowl.

3. Beat yogurt and cold water in small bowl until well combined. Drizzle over bean dip. Garnish with mint. Serve warm with pita bread.

SAUCED LITTLE SMOKIES (PRESSURE)

1 bottle (14 ounces)
  barbecue sauce

¾ cup grape jelly

½ cup packed brown sugar

½ cup ketchup

1 tablespoon prepared
  mustard

1 teaspoon Worcestershire
  sauce

3 packages (14 to
  16 ounces *each*)
  miniature cocktail
  franks

1 Coat inside of **CROCK-POT®** Express Crock Multi-Cooker with nonstick cooking spray.

2 Combine barbecue sauce, jelly, brown sugar, ketchup, mustard and Worcestershire sauce in large bowl; stir to blend. Reserve half of sauce. Add cocktail franks and remaining sauce to Express Crock. Secure lid. Press STEAM, set pressure to HIGH and time to 8 minutes. Make sure Steam Release Valve is in the "Seal" (closed) position. Press START/STOP.

3 Once cooking is complete, quick release pressure. Remove cocktail franks to reserved sauce using slotted spoon. Press BROWN/SAUTÉ on Express Crock; cook sauce, uncovered, on HIGH 5 minutes or until thickened. Pour thickened sauce over cocktail franks; toss to coat.

SAUCED LITTLE SMOKIES (SLOW COOK)

1 bottle (14 ounces)
  barbecue sauce

¾ cup grape jelly

½ cup packed brown sugar

½ cup ketchup

1 tablespoon prepared
  mustard

1 teaspoon Worcestershire
  sauce

3 packages (14 to
  16 ounces *each*)
  miniature cocktail
  franks

1 Coat inside of **CROCK-POT®** Express Crock Multi-Cooker with nonstick cooking spray.

2 Combine barbecue sauce, jelly, brown sugar, ketchup, mustard and Worcestershire sauce in Express Crock; stir to blend. Add cocktail franks; toss to coat. Secure lid. Press SLOW COOK, set temperature and time to LOW 3 to 4 hours or to HIGH 1 to 2 hours. Make sure Steam Release Valve is in the "Release" (open) position. Press START/STOP.

3 Once cooking is complete, remove cocktail franks to reserved sauce using slotted spoon. Press BROWN/SAUTÉ on Express Crock; cook sauce, uncovered, on HIGH 5 minutes or until thickened. Pour thickened sauce over cocktail franks; toss to coat.

PULLED PORK SLIDERS (PRESSURE)

1 teaspoon vegetable oil

1 boneless pork shoulder roast (3 pounds)*

1½ cups cola

¼ cup tomato paste

2 tablespoons packed brown sugar

2 teaspoons Worcestershire sauce

2 teaspoons spicy brown mustard

Hot pepper sauce

Salt

16 dinner rolls or potato rolls, split

Sliced pickles (optional)

*Cut any roast larger than 2½ pounds in half so it cooks completely.

1 Press BROWN/SAUTÉ on **CROCK-POT®** Express Crock Multi-Cooker; heat oil on HIGH. Add pork; cook, uncovered, 5 to 7 minutes or until browned on all sides. Pour cola over pork. Secure lid. Press MEAT/STEW, set pressure to HIGH and time to 55 minutes. Make sure Steam Release Valve is in the "Seal" (closed) position. Press START/STOP.

2 Once cooking is complete, natural release pressure 10 minutes. Release remaining pressure. Remove pork to large cutting board; shred with two forks. Let cooking liquid stand 5 to 10 minutes. Skim off and discard fat.

3 Press BROWN/SAUTÉ on Express Crock. Whisk tomato paste, brown sugar, Worcestershire sauce and mustard into cooking liquid. Bring to a boil; cook, uncovered, on HIGH 10 minutes or until thickened. Stir shredded pork back into Express Crock. Season with hot pepper sauce and salt. Serve on rolls with pickles, if desired.

PULLED PORK SLIDERS (SLOW COOK)

1 teaspoon vegetable oil

1 boneless pork shoulder roast (3 pounds)*

1 cup cola

¼ cup tomato paste

2 tablespoons packed brown sugar

2 teaspoons Worcestershire sauce

2 teaspoons spicy brown mustard

Hot pepper sauce

Salt

16 dinner rolls or potato rolls, split

Sliced pickles (optional)

*Cut any roast larger than 2½ pounds in half so it cooks completely.

1 Press BROWN/SAUTÉ on **CROCK-POT®** Express Crock Multi-Cooker; heat oil on HIGH. Add pork; cook 5 to 7 minutes until browned on all sides. Press START/STOP. Pour cola over pork. Secure lid. Press SLOW COOK, set temperature and time to LOW 7½ to 8 hours or to HIGH 3½ to 4 hours. Make sure Steam Release Valve is in the "Release" (open) position. Press START/STOP.

2 Once cooking is complete, remove pork to large cutting board and shred with two forks. Let cooking liquid stand 5 minutes. Skim off and discard fat.

3 Press BROWN/SAUTÉ on Express Crock. Whisk tomato paste, brown sugar, Worcestershire sauce and mustard into cooking liquid. Cook, uncovered, on HIGH 5 to 10 minutes or until thickened. Stir shredded pork back into Express Crock. Season with hot pepper sauce and salt. Serve on rolls with pickles, if desired.

SALSA-STYLE WINGS (PRESSURE)

2 tablespoons vegetable oil

1½ pounds chicken wings (about 18 wings)

2 cups salsa, plus additional for serving

¼ cup packed brown sugar

Sprigs fresh cilantro (optional)

1. Press BROWN/SAUTÉ on **CROCK-POT®** Express Crock Multi-Cooker; heat oil on HIGH. Add wings in batches; cook, uncovered, 3 to 4 minutes or until browned on all sides.

2. Combine 2 cups salsa and brown sugar in medium bowl; stir to blend. Pour over wings. Secure lid. Press POULTRY, set pressure to HIGH and time to 15 minutes. Make sure Steam Release Valve is in the "Seal" (closed) position. Press START/STOP.

3. Once cooking is complete, quick release pressure. Remove wings to large bowl. Let sauce stand 5 minutes. Skim off and discard fat. Press BROWN/SAUTÉ on Express Crock. Cook sauce, uncovered, on HIGH 5 minutes or until reduced by half. Pour sauce over wings. Serve with additional salsa; garnish with cilantro.

SALSA-STYLE WINGS (SLOW COOK)

MAKES 4 SERVINGS

2 tablespoons vegetable oil

1½ pounds chicken wings (about 18 wings)

2 cups salsa, plus additional for serving

¼ cup packed brown sugar

Sprigs fresh cilantro (optional)

1. Press BROWN/SAUTÉ on **CROCK-POT®** Express Crock Multi-Cooker; heat oil on HIGH. Add wings in batches; cook, uncovered, 3 to 4 minutes or until browned on all sides.

2. Combine 2 cups salsa and brown sugar in medium bowl; stir to blend. Pour over wings. Secure lid. Press SLOW COOK, set temperature and time to LOW 5 to 6 hours or to HIGH 2 to 3 hours. Make sure Steam Release Valve is in the "Release" (open) position. Press START/STOP.

3. Once cooking is complete, remove wings to large bowl. Let sauce stand 5 minutes. Skim off and discard fat. Press BROWN/SAUTÉ on Express Crock. Cook sauce, uncovered, on HIGH 5 minutes or until reduced by half. Pour sauce over wings. Serve with additional salsa; garnish with cilantro.

CHICKEN PÂTÉ (PRESSURE)

MAKES 8 TO 10 SERVINGS

1½ pounds chicken livers, trimmed of fat and membrane

1 cup chicken broth

1 small onion, thinly sliced

3 sprigs fresh thyme

2 cloves garlic, crushed

¼ teaspoon salt

3 tablespoons cold butter, cut into 4 pieces

2 tablespoons whipping cream

2 tablespoons dry sherry

½ shallot, minced

2 tablespoons chopped fresh Italian parsley

1 tablespoon sherry vinegar

⅛ teaspoon sugar

Black pepper

Melba toast or toast points

1 Rinse chicken livers and pat dry. Place chicken livers, broth, onion, thyme, garlic and salt in **CROCK-POT®** Express Crock Multi-Cooker. Secure lid. Press POULTRY, set pressure to HIGH and time to 15 minutes. Make sure Steam Release Valve is in the "Seal" (closed) position. Press START/STOP.

2 Once cooking is complete, quick release pressure. Remove and discard thyme sprigs. Strain remaining ingredients from Express Crock; cool slightly.

3 Remove chicken mixture to food processor or blender; pulse to coarsely chop livers. Add butter, one piece at a time, pulsing after each addition just to combine. Add cream and dry sherry; pulse to combine. Remove to small loaf pan, pressing plastic wrap to surface of pâté. Refrigerate overnight, tightly wrapped in additional plastic wrap.

4 To garnish pâté, combine shallot, parsley, sherry vinegar, sugar and pepper in small bowl; stir to blend. Spoon over pâté; serve with Melba toast.

CHICKEN PÂTÉ (SLOW COOK)

MAKES 8 TO 10 SERVINGS

1½ pounds chicken livers, trimmed of fat and membrane

1 small onion, thinly sliced

3 sprigs fresh thyme

1 tablespoon water

2 cloves garlic, crushed

¼ teaspoon salt

3 tablespoons cold butter, cut into 4 pieces

2 tablespoons whipping cream

2 tablespoons dry sherry

½ shallot, minced

2 tablespoons chopped fresh Italian parsley

1 tablespoon sherry vinegar

⅛ teaspoon sugar

Black pepper

Melba toast or toast points

1 Rinse chicken livers and pat dry. Place chicken livers, onion, thyme, water, garlic and salt in **CROCK-POT®** Express Crock Multi-Cooker. Secure lid. Press SLOW COOK, set temperature to LOW and time to 2 hours. Make sure Steam Release Valve is in the "Release" (open) position. Press START/STOP.

2 Once cooking is complete, remove and discard thyme sprigs. Strain remaining ingredients from Express Crock; cool slightly.

3 Remove chicken mixture to food processor or blender; pulse to coarsely chop livers. Add butter, one piece at a time, pulsing after each addition just to combine. Add cream and dry sherry; pulse to combine. Remove to small loaf pan, pressing plastic wrap to surface of pâté. Refrigerate overnight, tightly wrapped in additional plastic wrap.

4 To garnish pâté, combine shallot, parsley, sherry vinegar and sugar in small bowl; stir to blend. Spoon over pâté; serve with Melba toast.

BARBECUED MEATBALLS (PRESSURE)

- 2 pounds ground beef
- 1⅓ cups ketchup, divided
- 3 tablespoons seasoned dry bread crumbs
- 1 egg, lightly beaten
- 2 tablespoons dried minced onion
- ¾ teaspoon garlic salt
- ½ teaspoon black pepper
- Sliced green bell peppers
- 1 cup packed brown sugar
- 1 can (6 ounces) tomato paste
- ¼ cup soy sauce
- ¼ cup cider vinegar
- 1½ teaspoons hot pepper sauce

1 Combine beef, ⅓ cup ketchup, bread crumbs, egg, minced onion, garlic salt and black pepper in large bowl; mix well. Shape into 48 (1-inch) meatballs. Place meatballs in bottom of **CROCK-POT®** Express Crock Multi-Cooker. Add bell peppers.

2 Combine remaining 1 cup ketchup, brown sugar, tomato paste, soy sauce, vinegar and hot pepper sauce in medium bowl; stir to blend. Reserve half of sauce; pour remaining sauce into Express Crock over meatballs. Secure lid. Press BEANS/CHILI, set pressure to HIGH and time to 8 minutes. Make sure Steam Release Valve is in the "Seal" (closed) position. Press START/STOP.

3 Once cooking is complete, quick release pressure. Remove meatballs and bell peppers to reserved sauce. Press BROWN/SAUTÉ on Express Crock; cook sauce, uncovered, on HIGH 5 to 10 minutes or until thickened. Pour over meatballs and bell peppers; toss to coat.

BARBECUED MEATBALLS (SLOW COOK)

- 2 pounds ground beef
- 1⅓ cups ketchup, divided
- 3 tablespoons seasoned dry bread crumbs
- 1 egg, lightly beaten
- 2 tablespoons dried minced onion
- ¾ teaspoon garlic salt
- ½ teaspoon black pepper
- 1 cup packed brown sugar
- 1 can (6 ounces) tomato paste
- ¼ cup soy sauce
- ¼ cup cider vinegar
- 1½ teaspoons hot pepper sauce
- Sliced green bell peppers

1 Combine beef, ⅓ cup ketchup, bread crumbs, egg, minced onion, garlic salt and black pepper in large bowl; mix well. Shape mixture into 48 (1-inch) meatballs. Place meatballs in bottom of **CROCK-POT®** Express Crock Multi-Cooker.

2 Combine remaining 1 cup ketchup, brown sugar, tomato paste, soy sauce, vinegar and hot pepper sauce in medium bowl; stir to blend. Pour over meatballs. Secure lid. Press SLOW COOK, set temperature to LOW and time to 4 hours. Make sure Steam Release Valve is in the "Release" (open) position. Press START/STOP. Stir in bell peppers during last 15 minutes of cooking.

3 Once cooking is complete, remove meatballs and bell peppers to reserved sauce. Press BROWN/SAUTÉ on Express Crock; cook sauce, uncovered, on HIGH 5 to 10 minutes or until thickened. Pour over meatballs and bell peppers; toss to coat.

BRATS IN BEER (PRESSURE)

1½ pounds bratwurst
    (5 to 6 links)

1   can (12 ounces) amber
    ale or beer

1   onion, thinly sliced

2   tablespoons packed
    brown sugar

2   tablespoons red wine
    vinegar or cider vinegar

Spicy brown mustard

Cocktail rye bread

1 Combine bratwurst, ale, onion, brown sugar and vinegar in **CROCK-POT®** Express Crock Multi-Cooker. Secure lid. Press MEAT/STEW, set pressure to HIGH and time to 15 minutes. Make sure Steam Release Valve is in the "Seal" (closed) position. Press START/STOP.

2 Once cooking is complete, quick release pressure. Remove bratwurst to large cutting board; cut into ½-inch-thick slices. Remove onion from cooking liquid to small bowl using slotted spoon. Spread mustard on cocktail rye bread. Top with bratwurst slices and onion.

BRATS IN BEER (SLOW COOK)

MAKES 30 TO 36 APPETIZERS

1½ pounds bratwurst
    (5 to 6 links)

1   can (12 ounces) amber
    ale or beer

1   onion, thinly sliced

2   tablespoons packed
    brown sugar

2   tablespoons red wine
    vinegar or cider vinegar

Spicy brown mustard

Cocktail rye bread

1 Combine bratwurst, ale, onion, brown sugar and vinegar in **CROCK-POT®** Express Crock Multi-Cooker. Secure lid. Press SLOW COOK, set temperature to LOW and time to 4 hours. Make sure Steam Release Valve is in the "Release" (open) position. Press START/STOP.

2 Once cooking is complete, remove bratwurst to large cutting board; cut into ½-inch-thick slices. Remove onion from cooking liquid to small bowl using slotted spoon. Spread mustard on cocktail rye bread. Top with bratwurst slices and onion.

TIP: Choose a light-colored beer when cooking brats. Hearty ales can leave the meat tasting slightly bitter.

CHAPTER 2

SOUPS, CHILIES AND STEWS

TURKEY AND
VEGGIE SOUP
(page 66)

WEEKNIGHT
BEEF STEW
(page 80)

BLACK BEAN
MUSHROOM CHILI
(page 72)

SUMMER VEGETABLE STEW
(page 68)

BLACK AND WHITE CHILI
(page 58)

SPICY THAI COCONUT SOUP
(page 76)

HEARTY CHICKEN
TEQUILA SOUP (PRESSURE)

MAKES 4 SERVINGS

1½ pounds boneless, skinless chicken thighs

3 cups chicken broth

1 can (about 14 ounces) diced tomatoes with mild green chiles

1 cup frozen corn

1 small onion, cut into 8 wedges

¼ cup tequila

2 cloves garlic, minced

¼ cup sour cream

Chopped fresh cilantro

1 Combine chicken, broth, tomatoes, corn, onion, tequila and garlic in **CROCK-POT®** Express Crock Multi-Cooker. Secure lid. Press SOUP, set pressure to HIGH and time to 15 minutes. Make sure Steam Release Valve is in the "Seal" (closed) position. Press START/STOP.

2 Once cooking is complete, natural release pressure 10 minutes. Release remaining pressure. Remove chicken to large cutting board; shred with two forks. Stir shredded chicken into Express Crock. Ladle into individual bowls. Top each serving with sour cream; garnish with cilantro.

HEARTY CHICKEN
TEQUILA SOUP (SLOW COOK)

MAKES 4 SERVINGS

1 small onion, cut into 8 wedges

1 cup frozen corn

1 can (about 14 ounces) diced tomatoes with mild green chiles

2 cloves garlic, minced

2 tablespoons chopped fresh cilantro, plus additional for garnish

1½ pounds boneless, skinless chicken thighs

2 cups chicken broth

3 tablespoons tequila

¼ cup sour cream

1 Place onion wedges on bottom of **CROCK-POT®** Express Crock Multi-Cooker. Add corn, tomatoes, garlic and 2 tablespoons cilantro; stir to blend. Place chicken on top of tomato mixture. Pour broth and tequila over chicken and tomato mixture. Secure lid. Press SLOW COOK, set temperature to LOW and time to 8 hours. Make sure Steam Release Valve is in the "Release" (open) position. Press START/STOP.

2 Once cooking is complete, remove chicken to large cutting board; shred chicken with two forks. Stir shredded chicken into Express Crock. Ladle into individual bowls. Top each serving with sour cream; garnish with additional cilantro.

BLACK AND WHITE CHILI (PRESSURE)

1 tablespoon vegetable oil

1 cup chopped onion

1 pound boneless, skinless chicken breasts, cut into ¾-inch pieces

1 can (about 15 ounces) cannellini beans, rinsed and drained

1 can (about 15 ounces) black beans, rinsed and drained

1 can (about 14 ounces) stewed tomatoes

1 cup chicken broth

1 (1¼-ounce) packet Texas-style chili seasoning mix

1. Press BROWN/SAUTÉ on **CROCK-POT®** Express Crock Multi-Cooker; heat oil on HIGH. Add onion; cook and stir 3 minutes or until softened. Stir in chicken, beans, tomatoes, broth and seasoning mix until well blended. Secure lid. Press BEANS/CHILI, set pressure to HIGH and time to 7 minutes. Make sure Steam Release Valve is in the "Seal" (closed) position. Press START/STOP.

2. Once cooking is complete, natural release pressure 10 minutes. Release remaining pressure. Press BROWN/SAUTÉ on Express Crock; cook and stir chili on HIGH 3 to 5 minutes or until desired thickness is reached.

BLACK AND WHITE CHILI (SLOW COOK)

1 tablespoon vegetable oil

1 cup chopped onion

1 pound boneless, skinless chicken breasts, cut into ¾-inch pieces

1 can (about 15 ounces) cannellini beans, rinsed and drained

1 can (about 15 ounces) black beans, rinsed and drained

1 can (about 14 ounces) stewed tomatoes

2 tablespoons Texas-style chili seasoning mix

1. Press BROWN/SAUTÉ on **CROCK-POT®** Express Crock Multi-Cooker; heat oil on HIGH. Add onion; cook and stir 3 minutes or until softened. Stir in chicken, beans, tomatoes, broth and seasoning mix until well blended. Secure lid. Press SLOW COOK, set temperature to LOW and time to 4 to 4½ hours. Make sure Steam Release Valve is in the "Release" (open) position. Press START/STOP.

2. Once cooking is complete, press BROWN/SAUTÉ on Express Crock. Cook and stir chili on HIGH 3 to 5 minutes until desired thickness is reached.

SERVING SUGGESTION: For a change of pace, this delicious chili is excellent served over cooked rice or pasta.

HEARTY LENTIL STEW (PRESSURE)

- 2 cups cauliflower florets
- 1 package (16 ounces) frozen green beans
- 2 cups vegetable broth
- 1 can (15 ounces) chunky tomato sauce with garlic and herbs
- 1 cup dried lentils, rinsed and sorted
- 1 cup chopped onion
- 1 cup baby carrots
- 2 teaspoons ground cumin
- ¾ teaspoon ground ginger
- ½ cup peanuts

1 Combine cauliflower, green beans, broth, tomato sauce, lentils, onion, carrots, cumin and ginger in **CROCK-POT®** Express Crock Multi-Cooker. Secure lid. Press BEANS/CHILI, set pressure to HIGH and time to 8 minutes. Make sure Steam Release Valve is in the "Seal" (closed) position. Press START/STOP.

2 Once cooking is complete, natural release pressure 10 minutes. Release remaining pressure. Sprinkle each serving with peanuts.

HEARTY LENTIL STEW (SLOW COOK)

- 1 cup dried lentils, rinsed and sorted
- 1 package (16 ounces) frozen green beans
- 2 cups cauliflower florets
- 1 can (15 ounces) chunky tomato sauce with garlic and herbs
- 1 cup chopped onion
- 1 cup baby carrots, cut into halves crosswise
- 3 cups vegetable broth
- 2 teaspoons ground cumin
- ¾ teaspoon ground ginger
- ½ cup peanuts

1 Layer lentils, green beans, cauliflower, tomato sauce, onion and carrots in **CROCK-POT®** Express Crock Multi-Cooker. Combine broth, cumin and ginger in large bowl; stir to blend. Pour over vegetables. Secure lid. Press SLOW COOK, set temperature to LOW and time to 9 hours. Make sure Steam Release Valve is in the "Release" (open) position. Press START/STOP.

2 Once cooking is complete, sprinkle each serving with peanuts.

DOUBLE THICK
POTATO-CHEESE SOUP (PRESSURE)

2 pounds baking potatoes, cut into 1-inch cubes

2½ cups vegetable broth

1 cup chopped green onions, divided

¼ teaspoon garlic powder

⅛ teaspoon ground red pepper

1½ cups (6 ounces) shredded sharp Cheddar cheese

1 cup (8 ounces) sour cream

1 cup milk

Black pepper

1 Combine potatoes, broth, ½ cup green onions, garlic powder and ground red pepper in **CROCK-POT®** Express Crock Multi-Cooker. Secure lid. Press SOUP, set pressure to HIGH and time to 5 minutes. Make sure Steam Release Valve is in the "Seal" (closed) position. Press START/STOP.

2 Once cooking is complete, quick release pressure. Stir cheese, sour cream and milk into Express Crock until cheese is melted. Season with black pepper. Top with remaining ½ cup green onions.

DOUBLE THICK
POTATO-CHEESE SOUP (SLOW COOK)

MAKES 6 SERVINGS

2 pounds baking potatoes, cut into 1-inch cubes

2½ cups vegetable broth

1 cup chopped green onions, divided

¼ teaspoon garlic powder

⅛ teaspoon ground red pepper

1½ cups (6 ounces) shredded sharp Cheddar cheese

1 cup (8 ounces) sour cream

1 cup milk

Black pepper

1 Combine potatoes, broth, ½ cup green onions, garlic powder and ground red pepper in **CROCK-POT®** Express Crock Multi-Cooker. Secure lid. Press SLOW COOK, set temperature and time to LOW 8 hours or to HIGH 4 hours. Make sure Steam Release Valve is in the "Release" (open) position. Press START/STOP.

2 Once cooking is complete, stir in cheese, sour cream and milk. Cook, uncovered, on HIGH 5 minutes or until cheese is melted. Season with black pepper. Top with remaining ½ cup green onions.

SIMPLE BEEF CHILI (PRESSURE)

3 pounds ground beef

2 cans (about 14 ounces each) diced tomatoes

2 cans (about 15 ounces each) kidney beans, rinsed and drained

2 cups chopped onions

1 package (10 ounces) frozen corn

1 cup chopped green bell pepper

1 can (8 ounces) tomato sauce

1 cup beef broth

3 tablespoons chili powder

1 teaspoon garlic powder

½ teaspoon ground cumin

½ teaspoon dried oregano

Prepared corn bread (optional)

1 Press BROWN/SAUTÉ on **CROCK-POT®** Express Crock Multi-Cooker. Add beef; cook on HIGH 6 to 8 minutes, stirring to break up meat. Drain fat.

2 Add tomatoes, beans, onions, corn, bell pepper, tomato sauce, broth, chili powder, garlic powder, cumin and oregano to Express Crock. Secure lid. Press BEANS/CHILI, set pressure to HIGH and time to 10 minutes. Make sure Steam Release Valve is in the "Seal" (closed) position. Press START/STOP.

3 Once cooking is complete, natural release pressure 10 minutes. Release remaining pressure. Press BROWN/SAUTÉ on Express Crock; cook and stir chili on HIGH 5 minutes or until desired thickness. Serve with corn bread, if desired.

SIMPLE BEEF CHILI (SLOW COOK)

3 pounds ground beef

2 cans (about 14 ounces each) diced tomatoes

2 cans (about 15 ounces each) kidney beans, rinsed and drained

2 cups chopped onions

1 package (10 ounces) frozen corn

1 cup chopped green bell pepper

1 can (8 ounces) tomato sauce

3 tablespoons chili powder

1 teaspoon garlic powder

½ teaspoon ground cumin

½ teaspoon dried oregano

Prepared corn bread (optional)

1 Press BROWN/SAUTÉ on **CROCK-POT®** Express Crock Multi-Cooker. Add beef; cook on HIGH 6 to 8 minutes, stirring to break up meat. Drain fat.

2 Add tomatoes, beans, onions, corn, bell pepper, tomato sauce, chili powder, garlic powder, cumin and oregano to Express Crock. Secure lid. Press SLOW COOK, set temperature to LOW and time to 4 hours. Make sure Steam Release Valve is in the "Release" (open) position. Press START/STOP.

3 Once cooking is complete, serve with corn bread, if desired.

TURKEY AND VEGGIE SOUP (PRESSURE)

2 tablespoons butter, divided

8 ounces sliced mushrooms

½ cup chopped onion

4 cups turkey or chicken broth

1 red bell pepper, chopped

1 stalk celery, thinly sliced

1 carrot, thinly sliced

½ teaspoon dried thyme

2 cups chopped cooked turkey

4 ounces uncooked egg noodles

1 cup half-and-half

½ cup peas

¾ teaspoon salt

1. Press BROWN/SAUTÉ on **CROCK-POT®** Express Crock Multi-Cooker; melt 1 tablespoon butter on HIGH. Add mushrooms and onion; cook and stir 4 minutes or until onion is softened. Add broth, bell pepper, celery, carrot and thyme. Secure lid. Press POULTRY, set pressure to HIGH and time to 15 minutes. Make sure Steam Release Valve is in the "Seal" (closed) position. Press START/STOP.

2. Once cooking is complete, quick release pressure. Press BROWN/SAUTÉ on Express Crock; bring soup to a boil on HIGH, stirring to break up turkey. Add noodles; cook, uncovered, 8 minutes or until tender. Stir in half-and-half, peas, remaining 1 tablespoon butter and salt; cook, uncovered, 2 minutes or until heated through.

TURKEY AND VEGGIE SOUP (SLOW COOK)

2 tablespoons butter, divided

8 ounces sliced mushrooms

½ cup chopped onion

4 cups turkey or chicken broth

1 red bell pepper, chopped

½ cup thinly sliced celery

1 carrot, thinly sliced

½ teaspoon dried thyme

2 cups chopped cooked turkey

4 ounces uncooked egg noodles

1 cup half-and-half

½ cup frozen peas, thawed

¾ teaspoon salt

1. Press BROWN/SAUTÉ on **CROCK-POT®** Express Crock Multi-Cooker; melt 1 tablespoon butter on HIGH. Add mushrooms and onion; cook and stir 4 minutes or until onion is softened. Add broth, bell pepper, celery, carrot and thyme. Secure lid. Press SLOW COOK, set temperature to HIGH and time to 2½ hours. Make sure Steam Release Valve is in the "Release" (open) position. Press START/STOP.

2. Once cooking is complete, stir in turkey. Press BROWN/SAUTÉ on Express Crock; bring soup to a boil on HIGH, stirring to break up turkey. Add noodles; cook, uncovered, 8 minutes or until tender. Stir in half-and-half, peas, remaining 1 tablespoon butter and salt. Cook, uncovered, 2 minutes or until heated through.

SUMMER VEGETABLE STEW (PRESSURE)

1 cup vegetable broth

1 can (about 15 ounces) chickpeas, rinsed and drained

1 medium zucchini, cut into ½-inch pieces

1 summer squash, cut into ½-inch pieces

4 large plum tomatoes, cut into ½-inch pieces

1 cup frozen corn

1 teaspoon minced garlic

½ to 1 teaspoon dried rosemary

¼ cup grated Asiago or Parmesan cheese

1 tablespoon chopped fresh Italian parsley

Salt and black pepper

1 Combine broth, chickpeas, zucchini, squash, tomatoes, corn, garlic and rosemary in **CROCK-POT®** Express Crock Multi-Cooker; stir to blend. Secure lid. Press STEAM, set pressure to HIGH and time to 5 minutes. Make sure Steam Release Valve is in the "Seal" (closed) position. Press START/STOP.

2 Once cooking is complete, quick release pressure. Top each serving evenly with cheese and parsley. Season with salt and pepper.

SUMMER VEGETABLE STEW (SLOW COOK)

1 cup vegetable broth

1 can (about 15 ounces) chickpeas, rinsed and drained

1 medium zucchini, cut into ½-inch pieces

1 summer squash, cut into ½-inch pieces

4 large plum tomatoes, cut into ½-inch pieces

1 cup frozen corn

1 teaspoon minced garlic

½ to 1 teaspoon dried rosemary

¼ cup grated Asiago or Parmesan cheese

1 tablespoon chopped fresh Italian parsley

Salt and black pepper

1 Combine broth, chickpeas, zucchini, squash, tomatoes, corn, garlic and rosemary in **CROCK-POT®** Express Crock Multi-Cooker; stir to blend. Secure lid. Press SLOW COOK, set temperature and time to LOW 8 hours or to HIGH 5 hours. Make sure Steam Release Valve is in the "Release" (open) position. Press START/STOP.

2 Once cooking is complete, top each serving evenly with cheese and parsley. Season with salt and pepper.

ASIAN SUGAR SNAP PEA SOUP (PRESSURE)

- 2 tablespoons peanut or canola oil
- 2 green onions, chopped
- 1 medium carrot, thinly sliced
- 1 stalk celery, thinly sliced
- 1 leek, thinly sliced
- 3 cups vegetable broth
- 4 to 5 new potatoes, coarsely chopped
- 2 cups broccoli, cut into florets
- 1 tablespoon lemon juice
- 1 tablespoon soy sauce
- 1 teaspoon ground coriander
- 1 teaspoon ground cumin
- 1 teaspoon prepared horseradish
- $\frac{1}{8}$ teaspoon ground red pepper
- 1 cup fresh sugar snap peas, shelled, rinsed and drained
- 4 cups cooked brown rice

1 Press BROWN/SAUTÉ on **CROCK-POT®** Express Crock Multi-Cooker; heat oil on HIGH. Add green onions, carrots, celery and leek; cook and stir 3 minutes. Stir broth, potatoes, broccoli, lemon juice, soy sauce, coriander, cumin, horseradish and ground red pepper into Express Crock. Secure lid. Press SOUP, set pressure to HIGH and time to 5 minutes. Make sure Steam Release Valve is in the "Seal" (closed) position. Press START/STOP.

2 Once cooking is complete, quick release pressure. Stir in peas. Serve soup over rice.

ASIAN SUGAR SNAP PEA SOUP (SLOW COOK)

- 2 tablespoons peanut or canola oil
- 4 to 5 new potatoes, coarsely chopped
- 2 green onions, chopped
- 1 medium carrot, thinly sliced
- 1 stalk celery, thinly sliced
- 1 leek, thinly sliced
- 5 cups vegetable broth
- 2 cups broccoli, cut into florets
- 1 tablespoon lemon juice
- 1 tablespoon soy sauce
- 1 teaspoon ground coriander
- 1 teaspoon ground cumin
- 1 teaspoon prepared horseradish
- $\frac{1}{8}$ teaspoon ground red pepper
- 1 cup fresh sugar snap peas, shelled, rinsed and drained
- 4 cups cooked brown rice

1 Press BROWN/SAUTÉ on **CROCK-POT®** Express Crock Multi-Cooker; heat oil on HIGH. Add potatoes, green onions, carrot, celery and leek; cook and stir 3 minutes. Stir broth, broccoli, lemon juice, soy sauce, coriander, cumin, horseradish and ground red pepper into Express Crock. Secure lid. Press SLOW COOK, set temperature and time to LOW 5 to 6 hours or to HIGH 2 to 3 hours. Make sure Steam Release Valve is in the "Release" (open) position. Press START/STOP.

2 Once cooking is complete, stir in peas. Serve soup over rice.

BLACK BEAN
MUSHROOM CHILI (PRESSURE)

1 tablespoon vegetable oil

1 cup chopped onion

4 cloves garlic, minced

1 yellow or green bell pepper, finely diced

2 cups (8 ounces) sliced baby bella or button mushrooms

1 can (about 15 ounces) black beans, rinsed and drained

1 can (about 14 ounces) fire-roasted diced tomatoes

1 cup salsa

2 teaspoons ground cumin or chili powder

Sour cream (optional)

1 Press BROWN/SAUTÉ on **CROCK-POT**® Express Crock Multi-Cooker; heat oil on HIGH. Add onion, garlic and bell pepper; cook and stir 3 minutes or until softened. Add mushrooms, beans, tomatoes, salsa and cumin to Express Crock. Secure lid. Press BEANS/CHILI, set pressure to HIGH and time to 7 minutes. Make sure Steam Release Valve is in the "Seal" (closed) position. Press START/STOP.

2 Once cooking is complete, natural release pressure 10 minutes. Release remaining pressure. Ladle chili into shallow bowls. Top with sour cream, if desired.

BLACK BEAN
MUSHROOM CHILI (SLOW COOK)

1 tablespoon vegetable oil

1 cup chopped onion

4 cloves garlic, minced

1 yellow or green bell pepper, finely diced

2 cups (8 ounces) sliced baby bella or button mushrooms

1 can (about 15 ounces) black beans, rinsed and drained

1 can (about 14 ounces) fire-roasted diced tomatoes

1 cup salsa

2 teaspoons ground cumin or chili powder

Sour cream (optional)

1 Press BROWN/SAUTÉ on **CROCK-POT**® Express Crock Multi-Cooker; heat oil on HIGH. Add onion, garlic and bell pepper; cook and stir 3 minutes or until softened. Add mushrooms, beans, tomatoes, salsa and cumin to Express Crock; stir to blend. Secure lid. Press SLOW COOK, set temperature and time to LOW 5 to 6 hours or to HIGH 2½ to 3 hours. Make sure Steam Release Valve is in the "Release" (open) position. Press START/STOP.

2 Once cooking is complete, ladle chili into shallow bowls. Top with sour cream, if desired.

STEW PROVENÇAL (PRESSURE)

MAKES 8 SERVINGS

1 to 2 pork tenderloins (about 2 pounds), trimmed and cut into 1-inch pieces

3 tablespoons all-purpose flour

1 teaspoon salt

1 teaspoon dried thyme

½ teaspoon black pepper

2 tablespoons olive oil

2 cups beef broth

4 red potatoes, unpeeled and cut into cubes

2 cups frozen cut green beans, thawed

1 onion, chopped

2 cloves garlic, minced

Sprigs fresh thyme (optional)

1 Place pork, flour, salt, dried thyme and black pepper in large resealable food storage bag; toss to coat. Press BROWN/SAUTÉ on **CROCK-POT**® Express Crock Multi-Cooker; heat oil on HIGH. Add pork mixture; cook and stir 5 minutes or until browned. Add broth, potatoes, beans, onion and garlic; stir to blend. Secure lid. Press MEAT/STEW, set pressure to HIGH and time to 15 minutes. Make sure Steam Release Valve is in the "Seal" (closed) position. Press START/STOP.

2 Once cooking is complete, quick release pressure. Garnish with thyme sprigs.

STEW PROVENÇAL (SLOW COOK)

MAKES 8 SERVINGS

1 to 2 pork tenderloins (about 2 pounds), trimmed and cut into 1-inch pieces

3 tablespoons all-purpose flour

1 teaspoon salt

1 teaspoon dried thyme

½ teaspoon black pepper

2 tablespoons olive oil

2 cups beef broth

4 red potatoes, unpeeled and cut into cubes

2 cups frozen cut green beans, thawed

1 onion, chopped

2 cloves garlic, minced

Sprigs fresh thyme (optional)

1 Place pork, flour, salt, dried thyme and black pepper in large resealable food storage bag; toss to coat. Press BROWN/SAUTÉ on **CROCK-POT**® Express Crock Multi-Cooker; heat oil on HIGH. Add pork mixture; cook and stir 5 minutes or until browned. Add broth, potatoes, beans, onion and garlic; stir to blend. Secure lid. Press SLOW COOK, set temperature and time to LOW 8 to 10 hours or to HIGH 4 to 5 hours. Make sure Steam Release Valve is in the "Release" (open) position. Press START/STOP.

2 Once cooking is complete, garnish each serving with thyme sprigs.

SPICY THAI COCONUT SOUP (PRESSURE)

2 boneless, skinless chicken breasts (about 1 pound)

1 cup chicken broth

1 can (15 ounces) straw mushrooms, drained

1 can (13½ ounces) unsweetened coconut milk

1 can (about 8 ounces) baby corn, drained

2 tablespoons lime juice

1 tablespoon minced fresh ginger

½ to 1 teaspoon red curry paste*

¼ cup chopped fresh cilantro

Red curry paste can be found in jars in the Asian food section of large grocery stores. Spice levels can vary between brands. Start with ½ teaspoon, then add more as desired.

1 Combine chicken and broth in **CROCK-POT®** Express Crock Multi-Cooker. Secure lid. Press POULTRY, set pressure to HIGH and time to 20 minutes. Make sure Steam Release Valve is in the "Seal" (closed) position. Press START/STOP.

2 Once cooking is complete, natural release pressure 10 minutes. Release remaining pressure. Remove chicken to large cutting board; shred with two forks. Press BROWN/SAUTÉ on Express Crock. Stir shredded chicken, mushrooms, coconut milk, corn, lime juice, ginger and curry paste into Express Crock. Cook and stir on HIGH 3 to 5 minutes or until heated through. Sprinkle with cilantro just before serving.

SPICY THAI COCONUT SOUP (SLOW COOK)

3 cups coarsely shredded cooked chicken (about 12 ounces)

2 cups chicken broth

1 can (15 ounces) straw mushrooms, drained

1 can (13½ ounces) unsweetened coconut milk

1 can (about 8 ounces) baby corn, drained

1 tablespoon minced fresh ginger

½ to 1 teaspoon red curry paste*

2 tablespoons lime juice

¼ cup chopped fresh cilantro

Red curry paste can be found in jars in the Asian food section of large grocery stores. Spice levels can vary between brands. Start with ½ teaspoon, then add more as desired.

1 Combine chicken, broth, mushrooms, coconut milk, corn, ginger and curry paste in **CROCK-POT®** Express Crock Multi-Cooker. Secure lid. Press SLOW COOK, set temperature to HIGH and time to 2 to 3 hours. Make sure Steam Release Valve is in the "Release" (open) position. Press START/STOP.

2 Once cooking is complete, stir in lime juice and sprinkle with cilantro just before serving.

VEGETABLE SOUP WITH BEANS (PRESSURE)

- 4 cups vegetable broth
- 1 can (about 15 ounces) cannellini beans, rinsed and drained
- 1 can (about 14 ounces) diced tomatoes
- 16 baby carrots
- 1 medium onion, chopped
- 1 ounce dried oyster mushrooms, chopped
- 3 tablespoons tomato paste
- 2 teaspoons garlic powder
- 1 teaspoon dried basil
- 1 teaspoon dried oregano
- ½ teaspoon dried rosemary
- ½ teaspoon dried marjoram
- ½ teaspoon dried sage
- ½ teaspoon dried thyme
- ¼ teaspoon black pepper
- French bread slices, toasted (optional)

1 Combine broth, beans, tomatoes, carrots, onion, mushrooms, tomato paste, garlic powder, basil, oregano, rosemary, marjoram, sage, thyme and pepper in **CROCK-POT®** Express Crock Multi-Cooker; stir to blend. Secure lid. Press SOUP, set pressure to HIGH and time to 10 minutes. Make sure Steam Release Valve is in the "Seal" (closed) position. Press START/STOP.

2 Once cooking is complete, natural release pressure 10 minutes. Release remaining pressure. Serve with bread, if desired.

VEGETABLE SOUP WITH BEANS (SLOW COOK)

- 4 cups vegetable broth
- 1 can (about 15 ounces) cannellini beans, rinsed and drained
- 1 can (about 14 ounces) diced tomatoes
- 16 baby carrots
- 1 medium onion, chopped
- 1 ounce dried oyster mushrooms, chopped
- 3 tablespoons tomato paste
- 2 teaspoons garlic powder
- 1 teaspoon dried basil
- 1 teaspoon dried oregano
- ½ teaspoon dried rosemary
- ½ teaspoon dried marjoram
- ½ teaspoon dried sage
- ½ teaspoon dried thyme
- ¼ teaspoon black pepper
- French bread slices, toasted (optional)

1 Combine broth, beans, tomatoes, carrots, onion, mushrooms, tomato paste, garlic powder, basil, oregano, rosemary, marjoram, sage, thyme and pepper in **CROCK-POT®** Express Crock Multi-Cooker; stir to blend. Secure lid. Press SLOW COOK, set temperature and time to LOW 8 hours or to HIGH 4 to 5 hours. Make sure Steam Release Valve is in the "Release" (open) position. Press START/STOP.

2 Once cooking is complete, serve with bread, if desired.

WEEKNIGHT BEEF STEW (PRESSURE)

1½ pounds cubed beef stew meat

5 tablespoons all-purpose flour, divided

1 teaspoon dried thyme

1 teaspoon salt

1 teaspoon black pepper

1 tablespoon olive oil

2 medium russet potatoes (about 1 pound), cut into chunks

4 medium carrots, thickly sliced

1 large onion, cut into thin wedges

2 cups beef broth, divided

1. Place stew meat, 2 tablespoons flour, thyme, salt and pepper in large resealable food storage bag; shake to coat. Press BROWN/SAUTÉ on **CROCK-POT®** Express Crock Multi-Cooker; heat oil on HIGH. Add beef in batches; cook and stir 4 to 5 minutes or until browned on all sides.

2. Add potatoes, carrots and onion. Set aside ½ cup broth. Pour remaining 1½ cups broth over beef and vegetables. Secure lid. Press MEAT/STEW, set pressure to HIGH and time to 20 minutes. Make sure Steam Release Valve is in the "Seal" (closed) position. Press START/STOP.

3. Once cooking is complete, natural release pressure 10 minutes. Release remaining pressure. Press BROWN/SAUTÉ on Express Crock. Stir reserved broth into remaining 3 tablespoons flour in small bowl until smooth; whisk into stew. Cook, uncovered, on HIGH 5 to 10 minutes or until thickened.

WEEKNIGHT BEEF STEW (SLOW COOK)

1½ pounds cubed beef stew meat

5 tablespoons all-purpose flour, divided

1 teaspoon dried thyme

1 teaspoon salt

1 teaspoon black pepper

1 tablespoon olive oil

2 medium russet potatoes (about 1 pound), cut into chunks

4 medium carrots, thickly sliced

1 large onion, cut into thin wedges

3 cups beef broth, divided

1. Place stew meat, 2 tablespoons flour, thyme, salt and pepper in large resealable food storage bag; shake to coat. Press BROWN/SAUTÉ on **CROCK-POT®** Express Crock Multi-Cooker; heat oil on HIGH. Add beef in batches; cook and stir 4 to 5 minutes or until browned on all sides.

2. Add potatoes, carrots and onion. Set aside ½ cup broth. Pour remaining 2½ cups broth over beef and vegetables. Secure lid. Press SLOW COOK, set temperature and time to LOW 8 to 9 hours or to HIGH 4 to 5 hours. Make sure Steam Release Valve is in the "Release" (open) position. Press START/STOP.

3. Once cooking is complete and meat and vegetables are fork-tender, press BROWN/SAUTÉ on Express Crock. Stir reserved ½ cup broth into remaining 3 tablespoons flour in small bowl until smooth; whisk into stew. Cook, uncovered, on HIGH 5 to 10 minutes or until thickened.

CANNELLINI MINESTRONE SOUP (PRESSURE)

1 cup water

¼ cup dried cannellini beans, rinsed and sorted

1 teaspoon salt, divided

1 teaspoon black pepper, divided

1 tablespoon oil

1 cup chopped green onions

1 cup chopped celery

1 cup chopped carrots

2 cups vegetable broth

2 cups escarole, cut into ribbons

1 can (about 14 ounces) diced tomatoes

1 can (12 ounces) tomato-vegetable juice

1 cup chopped potatoes

2 tablespoons chopped fresh chives

1 tablespoon chopped fresh Italian parsley

2 ounces uncooked ditalini pasta

1 Combine water, beans, ½ teaspoon salt and ½ teaspoon pepper in **CROCK-POT®** Express Crock Multi-Cooker. Secure lid. Press BEANS/CHILI, set pressure to HIGH and time to 20 minutes. Make sure Steam Release Valve is in the "Seal" (closed) position. Press START/STOP.

2 Once cooking is complete, natural release pressure 10 minutes. Release remaining pressure. Drain beans; discard cooking liquid. Set aside.

3 Press BROWN/SAUTÉ on Express Crock; heat oil on HIGH. Add onions, celery and carrots; cook and stir 3 minutes. Add broth, escarole, tomatoes, vegetable juice, potatoes, chives, parsley, remaining ½ teaspoon salt and pepper to Express Crock. Bring to a boil; cook and stir 5 minutes. Add pasta. Bring to a boil; cook 10 minutes. Stir in beans.

CANNELLINI MINESTRONE SOUP (SLOW COOK)

4 cups chicken broth

2 cups escarole, cut into ribbons

1 can (about 14 ounces) diced tomatoes

1 can (12 ounces) tomato-vegetable juice

1 cup chopped green onions

1 cup chopped carrots

1 cup chopped celery

1 cup chopped potatoes

¼ cup dried cannellini beans, rinsed and sorted

2 tablespoons chopped fresh chives

1 tablespoon chopped fresh Italian parsley

¼ teaspoon salt

¼ teaspoon black pepper

2 ounces uncooked ditalini pasta

1 Combine broth, escarole, tomatoes, vegetable juice, green onions, carrots, celery, potatoes, beans, chives, parsley, salt and pepper in **CROCK-POT®** Express Crock Multi-Cooker; stir to blend. Secure lid. Press SLOW COOK, set temperature and time to LOW 6 to 8 hours or to HIGH 4 to 6 hours. Make sure Steam Release Valve is in the "Release" (open) position. Press START/STOP.

2 Once cooking is complete, stir in pasta. Press BROWN/SAUTÉ on Express Crock; cook, uncovered, 5 to 10 minutes or until pasta is tender.

VEGETABLE AND
RED LENTIL SOUP (PRESSURE)

- 2 tablespoons oil
- 1 red or yellow bell pepper, chopped
- ½ cup thinly sliced carrot
- 3 cups vegetable broth
- ½ cup dried red lentils, rinsed and sorted
- ½ teaspoon salt
- ½ teaspoon sugar
- ¼ teaspoon black pepper
- 2 medium zucchini or yellow summer squash, chopped
- 1 medium tomato, chopped
- 2 tablespoons chopped fresh basil or thyme
- ½ cup croutons (optional)

1 Press BROWN/SAUTÉ on **CROCK-POT®** Express Crock Multi-Cooker; heat oil on HIGH. Add bell pepper and carrot; cook and stir 3 minutes or until softened. Add broth, lentils, salt, sugar and black pepper to Express Crock; stir to blend. Secure lid. Press SOUP, set pressure to HIGH and time to 15 minutes. Make sure Steam Release Valve is in the "Seal" (closed) position. Press START/STOP.

2 Once cooking is complete, natural release pressure 10 minutes. Release remaining pressure. Press BROWN/SAUTÉ on Express Crock. Stir in zucchini and tomato; cook, uncovered, 5 minutes or until heated through. Sprinkle each serving with basil and croutons, if desired.

VEGETABLE AND
RED LENTIL SOUP (SLOW COOK)

- 1 can (about 14 ounces) vegetable broth
- 1 can (about 14 ounces) diced tomatoes
- 2 medium zucchini or yellow summer squash, chopped
- 1 red or yellow bell pepper, chopped
- ½ cup thinly sliced carrot
- ½ cup dried red lentils, rinsed and sorted
- ½ teaspoon salt
- ½ teaspoon sugar
- ¼ teaspoon black pepper
- 2 tablespoons chopped fresh basil or thyme
- ½ cup croutons (optional)

1 Combine broth, tomatoes, zucchini, bell pepper, carrot, lentils, salt, sugar and black pepper in **CROCK-POT®** Express Crock Multi-Cooker; stir to blend. Secure lid. Press SLOW COOK, set temperature and time to LOW 8 hours or to HIGH 4 hours. Make sure Steam Release Valve is in the "Release" (open) position. Press START/STOP.

2 Once cooking is complete, sprinkle each serving with basil and croutons, if desired.

CHAPTER 3

MAIN DISHES

ANDOUILLE AND
CABBAGE
(page 122)

SAFFRON-SCENTED
SHRIMP PAELLA
(page 98)

MEATBALLS AND
SPAGHETTI SAUCE
(page 106)

BONELESS PORK ROAST WITH GARLIC
(page 114)

HOT BEEF SANDWICHES AU JUS
(page 92)

SHREDDED CHICKEN TACOS
(page 118)

ITALIAN BRAISED SHORT RIBS IN RED WINE (PRESSURE)

- 2 tablespoons oil
- 3 pounds beef short ribs, trimmed of excess fat
- Salt and black pepper
- 2 large yellow onions, sliced
- 2 cloves garlic, minced
- 2 packages (8 ounces *each*) baby bella or cremini mushrooms, quartered
- 2 cups dry red wine
- 2 cups beef broth
- 2 teaspoons Italian seasoning
- 2 tablespoons water
- 2 tablespoons all-purpose flour
- Hot cooked mashed potatoes (optional)

1 Press BROWN/SAUTÉ on **CROCK-POT®** Express Crock Multi-Cooker; heat oil on HIGH. Season ribs with salt and pepper. Add ribs in batches; cook, uncovered, 6 to 8 minutes or until browned on all sides. Remove ribs to large plate.

2 Add onions to Express Crock; cook and stir 3 to 5 minutes or until tender. Add garlic, mushrooms, wine, broth and Italian seasoning; cook and stir 3 minutes. Add ribs. Secure lid. Press MEAT/STEW, set pressure to HIGH and time to 45 minutes. Make sure Steam Release Valve is in the "Seal" (closed) position. Press START/STOP.

3 Once cooking is complete, natural release pressure 10 minutes. Release remaining pressure. Remove ribs, mushrooms and onions to large serving platter; cover to keep warm. Press BROWN/SAUTÉ on Express Crock; heat cooking liquid on HIGH. Stir water into flour in small bowl; whisk into Express Crock. Cook, uncovered, 5 to 10 minutes or until thickened. Serve with mashed potatoes, if desired, and cooking liquid.

ITALIAN BRAISED SHORT RIBS IN RED WINE (SLOW COOK)

- 2 tablespoons oil
- 3 pounds beef short ribs, trimmed of excess fat
- Salt and black pepper
- 2 large yellow onions, sliced
- 2 cloves garlic, minced
- 2 packages (8 ounces *each*) baby bella or cremini mushrooms, quartered
- 2 cups dry red wine
- 2 cups beef broth
- 2 teaspoons Italian seasoning
- 2 tablespoons water
- 2 tablespoons all-purpose flour
- Hot cooked mashed potatoes (optional)

1 Press BROWN/SAUTÉ on **CROCK-POT®** Express Crock Multi-Cooker; heat oil on HIGH. Season ribs with salt and pepper. Add ribs in batches; cook, uncovered, 6 to 8 minutes or until browned on all sides. Remove to large plate.

2 Add onions to Express Crock; cook and stir 3 to 5 minutes or until tender. Add garlic, mushrooms, wine, broth and Italian seasoning; cook and stir 3 minutes. Add ribs. Secure lid. Press SLOW COOK, set temperature and time to LOW 10 to 12 hours or to HIGH 6 to 8 hours. Make sure Steam Release Valve is in the "Release" (open) position. Press START/STOP.

3 Once cooking is complete, remove ribs, mushrooms and onions to large serving platter; cover to keep warm. Press BROWN/SAUTÉ on Express Crock; heat cooking liquid on HIGH. Stir water into flour in small bowl; whisk into Express Crock. Cook, uncovered, 5 to 10 minutes or until thickened. Serve with mashed potatoes, if desired, and cooking liquid.

CHEESY SHRIMP ON GRITS (PRESSURE)

3½ cups chicken broth

1 cup quick-cooking grits

2 whole bay leaves

½ teaspoon salt

¼ cup (½ stick) butter, cubed

1 cup finely chopped green bell pepper

1 cup finely chopped red bell pepper

½ cup thinly sliced celery

1 cup green onions, chopped and divided

1 pound medium raw shrimp, peeled and deveined

1¼ teaspoons seafood seasoning

¼ teaspoon ground red pepper

2 cups (8 ounces) shredded sharp Cheddar cheese

¼ cup whipping cream or half-and-half

1 Combine broth, grits, bay leaves and salt in **CROCK-POT®** Express Crock Multi-Cooker. Secure lid. Press RICE/RISOTTO, set pressure to HIGH and time to 15 minutes. Make sure Steam Release Valve is in the "Seal" (closed) position. Press START/STOP.

2 Once cooking is complete, use natural release 10 minutes. Release remaining pressure. Remove grits to large bowl. Remove and discard bay leaves.

3 Press BROWN/SAUTÉ on Express Crock. Add butter; heat on HIGH until melted. Add bell peppers, celery and ½ cup green onions; cook and stir 5 minutes until softened. Stir in shrimp, seafood seasoning and ground red pepper; cook and stir 5 minutes or until shrimp are pink and opaque. Stir in cheese and cream; cook and stir 3 minutes or until cheese is melted and mixture is heated through. Divide grits into serving bowls; top evenly with shrimp mixture and remaining ½ cup green onions.

CHEESY SHRIMP ON GRITS (SLOW COOK)

1 cup finely chopped green bell pepper

1 cup finely chopped red bell pepper

½ cup thinly sliced celery

1 cup green onions, chopped and divided

¼ cup (½ stick) butter, cubed

1¼ teaspoons seafood seasoning

2 whole bay leaves

¼ teaspoon ground red pepper

1 cup quick-cooking grits

1 pound medium raw shrimp, peeled and deveined

2 cups (8 ounces) shredded sharp Cheddar cheese

¼ cup whipping cream or half-and-half

1 Coat inside of **CROCK-POT®** Express Crock Multi-Cooker with nonstick cooking spray. Add bell peppers, celery, ½ cup green onions, butter, seafood seasoning, bay leaves and ground red pepper. Secure lid. Press SLOW COOK, set temperature and time to LOW 4 hours or to HIGH 2 hours. Make sure Steam Release Valve is in the "Release" (open) position. Press START/STOP.

2   Meanwhile, prepare grits according to package directions.

3   Once cooking is complete, remove and discard bay leaves. Stir in shrimp. Press BROWN/SAUTÉ on Express Crock; cook, uncovered, on HIGH 5 minutes or until shrimp are pink and opaque. Stir in cheese, cream and remaining ½ cup green onions; cook 5 minutes or until cheese is melted. Serve over grits.

SERVING SUGGESTION: This dish is also delicious served over polenta.

HOT BEEF SANDWICHES AU JUS (PRESSURE)

2 cans (about 10 ounces *each*) beef broth

1 can (12 ounces) beer

2 envelopes (1 ounce *each*) dry onion soup mix

1 tablespoon minced garlic

2 teaspoons sugar

1 teaspoon dried oregano

4 pounds boneless beef bottom round roast, trimmed*

Crusty French rolls, sliced in half

Cut any roast larger than 2½ pounds in half so it cooks completely.

1 Combine broth, beer, dry soup mix, garlic, sugar and oregano in **CROCK-POT®** Express Crock Multi-Cooker; stir to blend. Add beef. Secure lid. Press MEAT/STEW, set pressure to HIGH and time to 1 hour. Make sure Steam Release Valve is in the "Seal" (closed) position. Press START/STOP.

2 Once cooking is complete, natural release pressure 10 minutes. Release remaining pressure. Remove beef to large cutting board; shred with two forks. Return beef to cooking liquid; stir to blend. Serve on rolls with cooking liquid for dipping.

HOT BEEF SANDWICHES AU JUS (SLOW COOK)

2 cans (about 10 ounces *each*) beef broth

1 can (12 ounces) beer

2 envelopes (1 ounce *each*) dry onion soup mix

1 tablespoon minced garlic

2 teaspoons sugar

1 teaspoon dried oregano

4 pounds boneless beef bottom round roast, trimmed*

Crusty French rolls, sliced in half

Cut any roast larger than 2½ pounds in half so it cooks completely.

1 Combine broth, beer, dry soup mix, garlic, sugar and oregano in **CROCK-POT®** Express Crock Multi-Cooker; stir to blend. Add beef. Secure lid. Press SLOW COOK, set temperature to HIGH and time to 4 to 6 hours. Make sure Steam Release Valve is in the "Release" (open) position. Press START/STOP.

2 Once cooking is complete, remove beef to large cutting board; shred with two forks. Return beef to cooking liquid; stir to blend. Serve on rolls with cooking liquid for dipping.

FAST-COOKED TURKEY BREAST (PRESSURE)

1 tablespoon dried parsley flakes

1 teaspoon garlic powder

1 teaspoon paprika

½ teaspoon salt

¼ teaspoon black pepper

1 turkey breast (5 to 7 pounds)

1 cup chicken broth

1 Combine parsley flakes, garlic powder, paprika, salt and pepper in small bowl; rub onto turkey. Pour broth into **CROCK-POT®** Express Crock Multi-Cooker; add turkey. Secure lid. Press POULTRY, set pressure to HIGH and time to 45 minutes. Make sure Steam Release Valve is in the "Seal" (closed) position. Press START/STOP.

2 Once cooking is complete, natural release pressure 5 minutes. Release remaining pressure. Remove turkey to large cutting board. Cover loosely with foil; let stand 10 to 15 minutes before slicing.

SLOW-COOKED TURKEY BREAST (SLOW COOK)

1 tablespoon dried parsley flakes

1 teaspoon garlic powder

1 teaspoon paprika

½ teaspoon salt

¼ teaspoon black pepper

1 turkey breast (5 to 7 pounds)*

1 Combine parsley flakes, garlic powder, paprika, salt and pepper in small bowl; rub onto turkey. Place turkey in **CROCK-POT®** Express Crock Multi-Cooker. Secure lid. Press SLOW COOK, set temperature and time to LOW 6 to 8 hours or to HIGH 2½ to 3 hours. Make sure Steam Release Valve is in the "Release" (open) position. Press START/STOP.

2 Once cooking is complete, remove turkey to large cutting board. Cover loosely with foil; let stand 10 to 15 minutes before slicing.

YANKEE POT ROAST
AND VEGETABLES (PRESSURE)

2 tablespoons olive oil

1 boneless beef chuck roast (about 2½ pounds), trimmed and cut into 1-inch pieces

Salt and black pepper

3 unpeeled medium baking potatoes (about 1 pound), cut into quarters

2 large carrots, cut into ¾-inch slices

2 stalks celery, cut into ¾-inch slices

1 medium onion, sliced

1 large parsnip, cut into ¾-inch slices

½ cup beef broth

2 whole bay leaves

1 teaspoon dried rosemary

½ teaspoon dried thyme

¼ cup water

2 tablespoons all-purpose flour

1 Press BROWN/SAUTÉ on **CROCK-POT®** Express Crock Multi-Cooker; heat oil on HIGH. Season beef with salt and pepper. Add beef in batches; cook, uncovered, 8 minutes or until browned on all sides. Remove to large plate.

2 Add beef, potatoes, carrots, celery, onion, parsnip, broth, bay leaves, rosemary and thyme to Express Crock. Secure lid. Press MEAT/STEW, set pressure to HIGH and time to 70 minutes. Make sure Steam Release Valve is in the "Seal" (closed) position. Press START/STOP.

3 Once cooking is complete, quick release pressure. Remove beef and vegetables to large serving platter. Remove and discard bay leaves. Let cooking liquid stand 5 minutes. Skim off and discard fat.

4 Press BROWN/SAUTÉ on Express Crock. Bring cooking liquid to a boil, uncovered, on HIGH. Stir water into flour in small bowl until smooth; whisk into cooking liquid. Cook and stir 5 minutes or until thickened.

YANKEE POT ROAST
AND VEGETABLES (SLOW COOK)

2 tablespoons olive oil

1 boneless beef chuck pot roast (about 2½ pounds), trimmed and cut into 1-inch pieces

Salt and black pepper

3 unpeeled medium baking potatoes (about 1 pound), cut into quarters

2 large carrots, cut into ¾-inch slices

2 stalks celery, cut into ¾-inch slices

1 medium onion, sliced

1 large parsnip, cut into ¾-inch slices

2 whole bay leaves

1 teaspoon dried rosemary

½ teaspoon dried thyme

½ cup beef broth

¼ cup water

2 tablespoons all-purpose flour

1 Press BROWN/SAUTÉ on **CROCK-POT®** Express Crock Multi-Cooker; heat oil on HIGH. Season beef with salt and pepper. Add beef in batches; cook, uncovered, 8 minutes or until browned on all sides. Remove to large plate.

2 Add potatoes, carrots, celery, onion, parsnip, bay leaves, rosemary and thyme to Express Crock. Place beef over vegetables. Pour broth over beef. Secure lid. Press SLOW COOK, set temperature to LOW and time to 8 to 9 hours. Make sure Steam Release Valve is in the "Release" (open) position. Press START/STOP.

3 Once cooking is complete and beef is fork-tender, remove beef and vegetables to large serving platter. Remove and discard bay leaves. Let cooking liquid stand 5 minutes. Skim off and discard fat.

4 Press BROWN/SAUTÉ on Express Crock. Bring cooking liquid to a boil, uncovered, on HIGH. Stir water into flour in small bowl until smooth; whisk into cooking liquid. Cook and stir 5 minutes or until thickened.

SAFFRON-SCENTED
SHRIMP PAELLA (PRESSURE)

MAKES 4 TO 6 SERVINGS

3 tablespoons olive oil, divided

25 large raw shrimp, peeled and deveined (with tails on)

1 teaspoon salt, divided

½ teaspoon white pepper

1½ cups chopped onions

4 cloves garlic, thinly sliced

1 cup roasted red bell pepper, diced

1 cup chopped tomato

1 whole bay leaf

1 large pinch saffron

1 cup dry white wine

4 cups uncooked rice

4 cups chicken broth

1 Press BROWN/SAUTÉ on **CROCK-POT®** Express Crock Multi-Cooker; heat 1 tablespoon oil on HIGH. Add shrimp, ½ teaspoon salt and white pepper; cook and stir 5 minutes or until shrimp are pink and opaque. Remove to large paper towel-lined plate. Set aside.

2 Add remaining 2 tablespoons oil, onions, garlic and remaining ½ teaspoon salt to Express Crock; cook and stir 5 minutes or until translucent. Add bell pepper, tomato, bay leaf and saffron; cook and stir 3 minutes. Add wine; cook and stir 5 minutes. Stir in rice and broth. Secure lid. Press RICE/RISOTTO, set pressure to HIGH and time to 6 minutes. Make sure Steam Release Valve is in the "Seal" (closed) position. Press START/STOP.

3 Once cooking is complete, natural release pressure 10 minutes. Release remaining pressure. Remove and discard bay leaf. Remove paella to serving bowls; top with shrimp.

SAFFRON-SCENTED
SHRIMP PAELLA (SLOW COOK)

MAKES 4 TO 6 SERVINGS

3 tablespoons olive oil, divided

25 large raw shrimp, peeled and deveined (with tails on)

½ teaspoon salt

½ teaspoon white pepper

1½ cups chopped onions

4 cloves garlic, thinly sliced

1 cup roasted red bell pepper, diced

1 cup chopped tomato

1 whole bay leaf

1 large pinch saffron

1 cup dry white wine

4 cups uncooked rice

8 cups chicken broth

1 Press BROWN/SAUTÉ on **CROCK-POT®** Express Crock Multi-Cooker; heat 1 tablespoon oil on HIGH. Add shrimp, ½ teaspoon salt and white pepper; cook and stir 5 minutes until shrimp are pink and opaque. Remove to large paper towel-lined plate. Set aside.

2 Add remaining 2 tablespoons oil, onions and garlic to Express Crock; cook and stir 5 minutes or until translucent. Add bell pepper, tomato, bay leaf and saffron; cook and stir 3 minutes. Add wine; cook and stir 5 minutes. Stir in rice and broth. Secure lid. Press SLOW COOK, set temperature to HIGH and time to 1 hour. Make sure Steam Release Valve is in the "Release" (open) position. Press START/STOP.

3 Once cooking is complete, remove and discard bay leaf. Remove paella to serving bowls; top with shrimp.

SHREDDED BEEF WRAPS (PRESSURE)

1 beef flank steak or
  beef skirt steak
  (1 to 1½ pounds)

1 cup beef broth

½ cup sun-dried tomatoes
  (not packed in oil),
  chopped

3 to 4 cloves garlic,
  minced

¼ teaspoon ground cumin

4 (8-inch) flour tortillas

  Optional toppings:
  shredded lettuce, diced
  tomatoes and shredded
  Monterey Jack cheese

1 Cut steak into quarters. Place steak, broth, sun-dried tomatoes, garlic and cumin in **CROCK-POT®** Express Crock Multi-Cooker. Secure lid. Press MEAT/STEW, set pressure to HIGH and time to 35 minutes. Make sure Steam Release Valve is in the "Seal" (closed) position. Press START/STOP.

2 Once cooking is complete, use natural release 10 minutes. Release remaining pressure. Remove steak to large cutting board; shred with two forks.

3 Press BROWN/SAUTÉ on Express Crock. Cook sauce, uncovered, 10 to 15 minutes or until thickened. Stir shredded beef back into Express Crock. Spoon beef mixture evenly onto tortillas. Top as desired.

SHREDDED BEEF WRAPS (SLOW COOK)

MAKES 4 SERVINGS

1 beef flank steak or
  beef skirt steak
  (1 to 1½ pounds)

1 cup beef broth

½ cup sun-dried tomatoes
  (not packed in oil),
  chopped

3 to 4 cloves garlic,
  minced

¼ teaspoon ground cumin

4 (8-inch) flour tortillas

  Optional toppings:
  shredded lettuce, diced
  tomatoes and shredded
  Monterey Jack cheese

1 Cut steak into quarters. Place steak, broth, sun-dried tomatoes, garlic and cumin in **CROCK-POT®** Express Crock Multi-Cooker. Secure lid. Press SLOW COOK, set temperature to LOW and time to 8 hours. Make sure Steam Release Valve is in the "Release" (open) position. Press START/STOP.

2 Once cooking is complete, remove steak to large cutting board; shred with two forks.

3 Press BROWN/SAUTÉ on Express Crock. Cook sauce, uncovered, 10 to 15 minutes or until thickened. Stir shredded beef back into Express Crock. Spoon beef mixture evenly onto tortillas. Top as desired.

BEER CHICKEN (PRESSURE)

MAKES 4 TO 6 SERVINGS

2 tablespoons olive oil

1 cut-up whole chicken (3 to 5 pounds)

10 new potatoes, halved

1 can (12 ounces) beer

4 medium carrots, chopped into 1-inch pieces

1 cup sliced celery

1 medium onion, chopped

1 tablespoon chopped fresh rosemary

1 teaspoon salt

½ teaspoon black pepper

2 tablespoons water

2 tablespoons all-purpose flour

1 Press BROWN/SAUTÉ on **CROCK-POT®** Express Crock Multi-Cooker; heat oil on HIGH. Add chicken in batches; cook, uncovered, 5 to 7 minutes or until browned. Remove to large paper towel-lined plate.

2 Add chicken, potatoes, beer, carrots, celery, onion, rosemary, salt, pepper and chicken to Express Crock. Secure lid. Press POULTRY, set pressure to HIGH and time to 15 minutes. Make sure Steam Release Valve is in the "Seal" (closed) position. Press START/STOP.

3 Once cooking is complete, quick release pressure. Remove chicken and potato mixture to large serving platter using slotted spoon; keep warm. Press BROWN/SAUTÉ on Express Crock. Stir water into flour in small bowl until smooth; whisk into cooking liquid. Cook, uncovered, on HIGH 10 to 15 minutes or until thickened. Serve chicken and vegetables with sauce.

BEER CHICKEN (SLOW COOK)

MAKES 4 TO 6 SERVINGS

2 tablespoons olive oil

1 cut-up whole chicken (3 to 5 pounds)

10 new potatoes, halved

1 can (12 ounces) beer

4 medium carrots, chopped into 1-inch pieces

1 cup sliced celery

1 medium onion, chopped

1 tablespoon chopped fresh rosemary

1 teaspoon salt

½ teaspoon black pepper

2 tablespoons water

2 tablespoons all-purpose flour

1 Press BROWN/SAUTÉ on **CROCK-POT®** Express Crock Multi-Cooker; heat oil on HIGH. Add chicken in batches; cook, uncovered, 5 to 7 minutes or until browned. Remove to large paper towel-lined plate.

2 Add chicken, potatoes, beer, carrots, celery, onion, rosemary, salt and pepper to Express Crock. Secure lid. Press SLOW COOK, set temperature to HIGH and time to 5 hours. Make sure Steam Release Valve is in the "Release" (open) position. Press START/STOP.

3 Once cooking is complete, remove chicken and potato mixture to large bowl using slotted spoon; keep warm. Press BROWN/SAUTÉ on Express Crock. Stir water into flour in small bowl until smooth; whisk into cooking liquid. Cook, uncovered, on HIGH 10 to 15 minutes or until thickened. Serve chicken and vegetables with sauce.

BARBECUE RIBS (PRESSURE)

3 tablespoons olive oil

2 racks pork baby back ribs, cut into 3- to 4-rib sections

2 small red onions, finely chopped

3 to 4 cloves garlic, minced

1 cup packed brown sugar

1 cup ketchup

½ cup cider vinegar

Juice of 1 lemon

2 tablespoons Worcestershire sauce

1 tablespoon hot pepper sauce

½ teaspoon chili powder

1 cup beef broth

1 Press BROWN/SAUTÉ on **CROCK-POT®** Express Crock Multi-Cooker; heat oil on HIGH. Add ribs in batches; cook, uncovered, 7 minutes or until browned. Remove ribs to large plate. Add onions and garlic; cook and stir 3 to 5 minutes or until softened. Stir in brown sugar, ketchup, vinegar, lemon juice, Worcestershire sauce, hot pepper sauce and chili powder; cook and stir 5 minutes. Remove half of sauce to large bowl; set aside.

2 Add ribs and broth to Express Crock; turn to coat. Secure lid. Press MEAT/STEW, set pressure to HIGH and time to 30 minutes. Make sure Steam Release Valve is in the "Seal" (closed) position. Press START/STOP.

3 Once cooking is complete, natural release pressure 10 minutes. Release remaining pressure. Remove ribs to large bowl with reserved sauce; turn to coat. Let cooking liquid stand 5 minutes; skim off and discard fat. Press BROWN/SAUTÉ on Express Crock. Cook sauce, uncovered, on HIGH 5 to 7 minutes or until thickened. Serve sauce with ribs.

BARBECUE RIBS (SLOW COOK)

3 tablespoons olive oil

2 small red onions, finely chopped

3 to 4 cloves garlic, minced

1 cup packed brown sugar

1 cup ketchup

½ cup cider vinegar

Juice of 1 lemon

2 tablespoons Worcestershire sauce

1 tablespoon hot pepper sauce

½ teaspoon chili powder

2 racks pork baby back ribs, cut into 3- to 4-rib sections

1 Press BROWN/SAUTÉ on **CROCK-POT®** Express Crock Multi-Cooker; heat oil on HIGH. Add ribs in batches; cook, uncovered, 7 minutes or until browned. Remove ribs to large paper towel-lined plate. Add onions and garlic; cook and stir 3 to 5 minutes or until softened. Stir in brown sugar, ketchup, vinegar, lemon juice, Worcestershire sauce, hot pepper sauce and chili powder; cook and stir 5 minutes. Remove half of sauce to large bowl; set aside.

2 Add ribs to Express Crock; turn to coat. Secure lid. Press SLOW COOK, set temperature and time to LOW 7 to 9 hours or to HIGH 4 to 6 hours. Make sure Steam Release Valve is in the "Release" (open) position. Press START/STOP.

3 Once cooking is complete, remove ribs to large bowl with reserved sauce; turn to coat. Skim off and discard fat from cooking liquid. Press BROWN/SAUTÉ on Express Crock. Cook sauce, uncovered, on HIGH 5 to 7 minutes or until thickened. Serve sauce with ribs.

MEATBALLS AND
SPAGHETTI SAUCE (PRESSURE)

2 pounds ground beef

1 cup plain dry bread
   crumbs

1 onion, chopped

2 eggs, beaten

¼ cup minced fresh Italian
   parsley

4 teaspoons minced garlic,
   divided

½ teaspoon ground
   mustard

½ teaspoon black pepper

2 tablespoons olive oil,
   divided

1 can (about 14 ounces)
   whole tomatoes

1 can (about 14 ounces)
   tomato sauce

½ cup chopped fresh basil

1 teaspoon sugar

   Salt and black pepper

   Hot cooked spaghetti

1 Combine beef, bread crumbs, onion, eggs, parsley, 2 teaspoons garlic, ground mustard and ½ teaspoon pepper in large bowl; mix well. Shape mixture into 1½-inch meatballs. Press BROWN/SAUTÉ on **CROCK-POT®** Express Crock Multi-Cooker; heat 1 tablespoon oil on HIGH. Add half of meatballs; cook, uncovered, 6 to 8 minutes or until browned on all sides. Remove to large paper towel-lined plate. Repeat with remaining meatballs and oil.

2 Combine tomatoes, tomato sauce, basil, remaining 2 teaspoons garlic, sugar, salt and pepper in Express Crock; stir to blend. Add meatballs; turn to coat. Secure lid. Press MEAT/STEW, set pressure to HIGH and time to 15 minutes. Make sure Steam Release Valve is in the "Seal" (closed) position. Press START/STOP.

3 Once cooking is complete, quick release pressure. Remove meatballs to large bowl. Press BROWN/SAUTÉ on Express Crock; cook sauce, uncovered, on HIGH 10 minutes or until thickened. Serve sauce and meatballs over spaghetti.

MEATBALLS AND
SPAGHETTI SAUCE (SLOW COOK)

2 pounds ground beef

1 cup plain dry bread
   crumbs

1 onion, chopped

2 eggs, beaten

¼ cup minced fresh Italian
   parsley

4 teaspoons minced garlic,
   divided

½ teaspoon ground
   mustard

½ teaspoon black pepper

2 tablespoons olive oil,
   divided

1 can (28 ounces) whole
   tomatoes

½ cup chopped fresh basil

1 teaspoon sugar

   Salt and black pepper

   Hot cooked spaghetti

1. Combine beef, bread crumbs, onion, eggs, parsley, 2 teaspoons garlic, ground mustard and ½ teaspoon pepper in large bowl; mix well. Shape mixture into 1½-inch meatballs. Press BROWN/SAUTÉ on **CROCK-POT®** Express Crock Multi-Cooker; heat 1 tablespoon oil on HIGH. Add half of meatballs; cook, uncovered, 6 to 8 minutes or until browned on all sides. Remove to large paper towel-lined plate. Repeat with remaining meatballs and 1 tablespoon oil.

2. Combine tomatoes, basil, remaining 2 teaspoons garlic, sugar, salt and pepper in Express Crock; stir to blend. Add meatballs; turn to coat. Secure lid. Press SLOW COOK, set temperature and time to LOW 3 to 5 hours or to HIGH 2 to 4 hours. Make sure Steam Release Valve is in the "Release" (open) position. Press START/STOP.

3. Once cooking is complete, remove meatballs to large bowl. Press BROWN/SAUTÉ on Express Crock; cook sauce, uncovered, on HIGH 10 minutes or until thickened. Serve sauce and meatballs over spaghetti.

COCONUT-CURRY
CHICKEN THIGHS (PRESSURE)

- 1 tablespoon olive oil
- 8 chicken thighs (about 2 to 2½ pounds)
- ½ teaspoon salt
- ¼ teaspoon black pepper
- 1 medium onion, chopped
- 1 medium red bell pepper, chopped
- 3 cloves garlic, minced
- 1 tablespoon grated fresh ginger
- 1 can (about 13 ounces) unsweetened coconut milk
- 3 tablespoons honey
- 1 tablespoon Thai red curry paste
- 2 teaspoons Thai roasted red chili paste
- 2 tablespoons chopped fresh cilantro (optional)
- ½ cup chopped cashew nuts (optional)

1 Press BROWN/SAUTÉ on **CROCK-POT®** Express Crock Multi-Cooker; heat oil on HIGH. Season chicken with salt and black pepper. Add chicken in batches; cook, uncovered, 6 to 8 minutes or until browned. Remove to large plate.

2 Pour off all but 1 tablespoon fat from Express Crock; heat on HIGH. Add onion, bell pepper, garlic and ginger; cook and stir 2 minutes or until vegetables are softened. Stir in coconut milk, honey, curry paste and chili paste until smooth. Add chicken; turn to coat. Secure lid. Press POULTRY, set pressure to HIGH and time to 15 minutes. Make sure Steam Release Valve is in the "Seal" (closed) position. Press START/STOP.

3 Once cooking is complete, quick release pressure. Remove chicken to large serving plate. Press BROWN/SAUTÉ on Express Crock; cook sauce, uncovered, on HIGH 5 minutes or until thickened. Serve chicken with sauce. Garnish each serving with cilantro and cashews.

COCONUT-CURRY
CHICKEN THIGHS (SLOW COOK)

- 1 tablespoon olive oil
- 8 chicken thighs (about 2 to 2½ pounds)
- ½ teaspoon salt
- ¼ teaspoon black pepper
- 1 medium onion, chopped
- 1 medium red bell pepper, chopped
- 3 cloves garlic, minced
- 1 tablespoon grated fresh ginger
- 1 can (about 13 ounces) unsweetened coconut milk
- 3 tablespoons honey
- 1 tablespoon Thai red curry paste
- 2 teaspoons Thai roasted red chili paste
- 2 tablespoons chopped fresh cilantro (optional)
- ½ cup chopped cashew nuts (optional)

1 Press BROWN/SAUTÉ on **CROCK-POT®** Express Crock Multi-Cooker; heat oil on HIGH. Season chicken with salt and black pepper. Add chicken in batches; cook, uncovered, 6 to 8 minutes or until browned. Remove to large plate.

2 Pour off all but 1 tablespoon fat from Express Crock; heat on HIGH. Add onion, bell pepper, garlic and ginger; cook and stir 2 minutes or until vegetables are softened. Add chicken; turn to coat. Combine coconut milk, honey, curry paste and chili paste in medium bowl; stir to blend. Pour coconut mixture over chicken. Secure lid. Press SLOW COOK, set temperature to LOW and time to 4 hours. Make sure Steam Release Valve is in the "Release" (open) position. Press START/STOP.

3 Once cooking is complete, serve chicken with sauce. Garnish each serving with cilantro and cashews.

TOMATO AND WINE BRISKET (PRESSURE)

MAKES 8 SERVINGS

1 tablespoon olive oil

1 beef brisket (3 to 3½ pounds), trimmed*

¾ teaspoon salt, divided

¼ teaspoon black pepper

1 large red onion, sliced

½ cup dry red wine

1 can (28 ounces) diced tomatoes with basil, oregano and garlic

Cut any roast larger than 2½ pounds in half so it cooks completely.

1 Press BROWN/SAUTÉ on **CROCK-POT®** Express Crock Multi-Cooker; heat oil on HIGH. Season beef with ½ teaspoon salt and pepper. Add beef; cook, uncovered, 10 minutes or until browned on all sides. Remove beef to large plate.

2 Add onion; cook and stir 3 minutes or until softened. Pour in wine; cook, uncovered, 3 minutes or until wine is mostly evaporated. Add tomatoes and remaining ¼ teaspoon salt. Place beef on top of vegetable mixture; press down slightly. Secure lid. Press MEAT/STEW, set pressure to HIGH and time to 1 hour, 15 minutes. Make sure Steam Release Valve is in the "Seal" (closed) position. Press START/STOP.

3 Once cooking is complete, natural release pressure 10 minutes. Release remaining pressure. Remove beef to large cutting board; cover loosely with foil. Let stand 15 minutes before slicing. Press BROWN/SAUTÉ on Express Crock; cook sauce, uncovered, on HIGH 5 minutes or until thickened. Serve sauce over brisket.

TOMATO AND WINE BRISKET (SLOW COOK)

MAKES 8 SERVINGS

1 tablespoon olive oil

1 beef brisket (3 to 3½ pounds), trimmed*

¾ teaspoon salt, divided

¼ teaspoon black pepper

1 large red onion, sliced

½ cup dry red wine

1 can (28 ounces) diced tomatoes with basil, oregano and garlic

Cut any roast larger than 2½ pounds in half so it cooks completely.

1 Press BROWN/SAUTÉ on **CROCK-POT®** Express Crock Multi-Cooker; heat oil on HIGH. Season beef with ½ teaspoon salt and pepper. Add beef; cook, uncovered, 10 minutes or until browned on all sides. Remove beef to large plate.

2 Add onion; cook and stir 3 minutes or until softened. Pour in wine; cook, uncovered, 3 minutes or until wine is mostly evaporated. Add tomatoes and remaining ¼ teaspoon salt. Place beef on top of vegetable mixture; press down slightly. Secure lid. Press SLOW COOK, set temperature to LOW and time to 7 to 8 hours. Make sure Steam Release Valve is in the "Release" (open) position. Press START/STOP.

3 Once cooking is complete, remove beef to large cutting board; cover loosely with foil. Let stand 15 minutes before slicing. Press BROWN/SAUTÉ on Express Crock; cook sauce, uncovered, on HIGH 5 minutes or until thickened. Serve sauce over brisket.

SPAGHETTI SQUASH WITH SHRIMP AND VEGGIES (PRESSURE)

- 2 cups water
- 1 spaghetti squash (3 pounds)
- 2 tablespoons olive oil
- ½ pound medium shrimp, peeled and deveined (with tails on)
- 1 orange or red bell pepper, cut into 1-inch squares
- 4 cups fresh baby spinach
- ½ cup julienned sun-dried tomatoes (not packed in oil)
- 3 tablespoons prepared pesto
- 1 teaspoon salt
- ¼ cup grated Parmesan cheese (optional)

1 Place rack and water in **CROCK-POT®** Express Crock Multi-Cooker. Pierce squash evenly 10 times with knife; place on rack. Secure lid. Press STEAM, set pressure to HIGH and time to 30 minutes. Make sure Steam Release Valve is in the "Seal" (closed) position. Press START/STOP.

2 Once cooking is complete, quick release pressure. Remove squash to large cutting board; let stand until cool enough to handle. Discard water in Express Crock.

3 Press BROWN/SAUTÉ on Express Crock; heat oil on HIGH. Add shrimp; cook, uncovered, 5 minutes or until pink and opaque. Remove to small plate. Add bell pepper to Express Crock; cook and stir 5 minutes. Add spinach, tomatoes, pesto and salt; cook 3 to 5 minutes until spinach is wilted.

4 Cut squash in half lengthwise. Remove and discard seeds and fibers; scoop pulp into shreds. Place squash shreds in large bowl; stir in spinach mixture. Spoon squash mixture into individual bowls; top with shrimp and cheese, if desired.

SPAGHETTI SQUASH WITH SHRIMP AND VEGGIES (SLOW COOK)

- 2 cups water
- 1 spaghetti squash (3 pounds)
- 4 cups fresh baby spinach
- 1 orange or red bell pepper, cut into 1-inch squares
- ½ cup julienned sun-dried tomatoes (not packed in oil)
- 3 tablespoons prepared pesto
- 2 tablespoons olive oil
- 1 teaspoon salt
- 1 pound cooked medium shrimp (with tails on)
- ¼ cup grated Parmesan cheese (optional)

1. Place rack and water in **CROCK-POT®** Express Crock Multi-Cooker. Pierce squash evenly 10 times with knife; place on rack. Secure lid. Press SLOW COOK, set temperature to HIGH and time to 2½ hours. Make sure Steam Release Valve is in the "Release" (open) position. Press START/STOP.

2. Once cooking is complete, remove squash to large cutting board; let stand until cool enough to handle.

3. Pour out all but 2 tablespoons water from Express Crock. Add spinach, bell pepper, tomatoes, pesto, oil and salt; stir to blend. Secure lid. Press SLOW COOK, set temperature to HIGH and time to 5 minutes. Make sure Steam Release Valve is in the "Release" (open) position. Press START/STOP.

4. Once cooking is complete, cut squash in half lengthwise. Remove and discard seeds and fibers. Scoop pulp into shreds; toss well with spinach mixture. Place shrimp on top of squash mixture. Secure lid. Press SLOW COOK, set temperature to HIGH and time to 15 minutes. Make sure Steam Release Valve is in the "Release" (open) position. Press START/STOP.

5. Once cooking is complete and shrimp are pink and opaque, top each serving with cheese, if desired.

BONELESS PORK ROAST WITH GARLIC (PRESSURE)

1 boneless pork loin roast (2 to 2½ pounds)

Salt and black pepper

3 tablespoons olive oil, divided

4 cloves garlic, minced

¼ cup chopped fresh rosemary

½ lemon, cut into ⅛- to ¼-inch slices

½ cup chicken broth

¼ cup dry white wine

1 Season pork with salt and pepper. Combine 2 tablespoons oil, garlic and rosemary in small bowl; stir to blend. Rub over pork. Roll and tie pork with kitchen string. Tuck lemon slices under string and into ends of roast.

2 Press BROWN/SAUTÉ on **CROCK-POT®** Express Crock Multi-Cooker; heat remaining 1 tablespoon oil on HIGH. Add pork; cook 6 to 8 minutes or until browned on all sides. Pour broth and wine over pork. Secure lid. Press MEAT/STEW, set pressure to HIGH and time to 20 minutes. Make sure Steam Release Valve is in the "Seal" (closed) position. Press START/STOP.

3 Once cooking is complete, natural release pressure 10 minutes. Release remaining pressure. Remove roast to large cutting board. Cover loosely with foil; let stand 10 to 15 minutes before removing kitchen string and slicing. Serve roast with cooking liquid.

BONELESS PORK ROAST WITH GARLIC (SLOW COOK)

1 boneless pork loin roast (2 to 2½ pounds)

Salt and black pepper

3 tablespoons olive oil, divided

4 cloves garlic, minced

¼ cup chopped fresh rosemary

½ lemon, cut into ⅛- to ¼-inch slices

½ cup chicken broth

¼ cup dry white wine

1 Season pork with salt and pepper. Combine 2 tablespoons oil, garlic and rosemary in small bowl; stir to blend. Rub over pork. Roll and tie pork with kitchen string. Tuck lemon slices under string and into ends of roast.

2 Press BROWN/SAUTÉ on **CROCK-POT®** Express Crock Multi-Cooker; heat remaining 1 tablespoon oil on HIGH. Add pork; cook 6 to 8 minutes or until browned on all sides. Pour broth and wine over pork. Secure lid. Press SLOW COOK, set temperature and time to LOW 8 to 9 hours or to HIGH 3½ to 4 hours. Make sure Steam Release Valve is in the "Release" (open) position. Press START/STOP.

3 Once cooking is complete, remove roast to large cutting board. Cover loosely with foil; let stand 10 to minutes before removing kitchen string and slicing. Serve roast with cooking liquid.

POT ROAST WITH BACON AND MUSHROOMS (PRESSURE)

6 slices bacon

1 boneless beef chuck roast (2½ to 3 pounds), trimmed*

¾ teaspoon salt, divided

¼ teaspoon black pepper

¾ cup chopped shallots

8 ounces sliced white mushrooms

¼ ounce dried porcini mushrooms (optional)

4 cloves garlic, minced

1 teaspoon dried oregano

1 cup beef broth

2 tablespoons tomato paste

Roasted Cauliflower (recipe follows, optional)

Cut any roast larger than 2½ pounds in half so it cooks completely.

1 Press BROWN/SAUTÉ on **CROCK-POT®** Express Crock Multi-Cooker. Add bacon; cook and stir until crisp. Remove to paper towel-lined plate using slotted spoon; crumble. Set aside.

2 Season roast with ½ teaspoon salt and pepper. Add roast to Express Crock; cook, uncovered, on HIGH 8 minutes or until browned. Remove to large plate. Add shallots, white mushrooms, porcini mushrooms, if desired, garlic, oregano and remaining ¼ teaspoon salt; cook, uncovered, 3 to 4 minutes or until vegetables are softened.

3 Place roast on top of vegetables in Express Crock. Combine broth and tomato paste in small bowl; stir to blend. Pour broth mixture over roast. Secure lid. Press MEAT/STEW, set pressure to HIGH and time to 70 minutes. Make sure Steam Release Valve is in the "Seal" (closed) position. Press START/STOP.

4 Meanwhile, prepare Roasted Cauliflower, if desired.

5 Once cooking is complete, natural release pressure 10 minutes. Release remaining pressure. Remove roast to large cutting board. Let stand 10 minutes before slicing. Top each serving with vegetables, cooking liquid and bacon. Serve with Roasted Cauliflower, if desired.

POT ROAST WITH BACON AND MUSHROOMS (SLOW COOK)

6 slices bacon

1 boneless beef chuck roast (2½ to 3 pounds), trimmed*

¾ teaspoon salt, divided

¼ teaspoon black pepper

¾ cup chopped shallots

8 ounces sliced white mushrooms

¼ ounce dried porcini mushrooms (optional)

4 cloves garlic, minced

1 teaspoon dried oregano

1 cup beef broth

2 tablespoons tomato paste

Roasted Cauliflower (recipe follows, optional)

Cut any roast larger than 2½ pounds in half so it cooks completely.

1. Press BROWN/SAUTÉ on **CROCK-POT®** Express Crock Multi-Cooker. Add bacon; cook and stir on HIGH until crisp. Remove to paper towel-lined plate using slotted spoon; crumble. Set aside.

2. Season roast with ½ teaspoon salt and pepper. Add roast to Express Crock; cook, uncovered, on HIGH 8 minutes or until browned. Remove to large plate. Add shallots, white mushrooms, porcini mushrooms, if desired, garlic, oregano and remaining ¼ teaspoon salt; cook and stir 3 to 4 minutes or until vegetables are softened.

3. Place roast on top of vegetables in Express Crock. Combine broth and tomato paste in small bowl; stir to blend. Pour broth mixture over roast. Secure lid. Press SLOW COOK, set temperature to LOW and time to 8 hours. Make sure Steam Release Valve is in the "Release" (open) position. Press START/STOP.

4. Meanwhile, prepare Roasted Cauliflower, if desired.

5. Once cooking is complete, remove roast to large cutting board. Let stand 10 minutes before slicing. Top each serving with vegetables, cooking liquid and bacon. Serve with Roasted Cauliflower, if desired.

ROASTED CAULIFLOWER: Preheat oven to 375°F. Break 1 head cauliflower into florets onto large baking sheet; coat with olive oil. Roast 20 minutes. Turn; roast 15 minutes. Makes 6 servings.

SHREDDED CHICKEN TACOS (PRESSURE)

2 pounds boneless, skinless chicken thighs

½ cup prepared mango salsa, plus additional for serving

Lettuce (optional)

8 (6-inch) yellow corn tortillas, warmed

1 Coat inside of **CROCK-POT®** Express Crock Multi-Cooker with nonstick cooking spray. Add chicken and ½ cup salsa. Secure lid. Press POULTRY, set pressure to HIGH and time to 15 minutes. Make sure Steam Release Valve is in the "Seal" (closed) position. Press START/STOP.

2 Once cooking is complete, natural release pressure 10 minutes. Release remaining pressure. Remove chicken to large cutting board; shred with two forks. Stir shredded chicken back into Express Crock. To serve, divide chicken and lettuce, if desired, evenly among tortillas. Serve with additional salsa.

SHREDDED CHICKEN TACOS (SLOW COOK)

MAKES 4 SERVINGS

2 pounds boneless, skinless chicken thighs

¾ cup prepared mango salsa, plus additional for serving

Lettuce (optional)

8 (6-inch) yellow corn tortillas, warmed

1 Coat inside of **CROCK-POT®** Express Crock Multi-Cooker with nonstick cooking spray. Add chicken and ½ cup salsa. Secure lid. Press SLOW COOK, set temperature and time to LOW 4 to 5 hours or to HIGH 2½ to 3 hours. Make sure Steam Release Valve is in the "Release" (open) position. Press START/STOP.

2 Once cooking is complete, remove chicken to large cutting board; shred with two forks. Stir shredded chicken back into Express Crock. To serve, divide chicken and lettuce, if desired, evenly among tortillas. Serve with additional salsa.

BRAISED LAMB SHANKS (PRESSURE)

2 tablespoons olive oil

4 (12- to 14-ounce) lamb shanks

¾ teaspoon salt, divided

¼ teaspoon black pepper

1 medium onion, chopped

2 stalks celery, chopped

2 carrots, chopped

6 cloves garlic, minced

1 teaspoon dried basil

1 can (about 14 ounces) diced tomatoes

2 tablespoons tomato paste

Chopped fresh Italian parsley (optional)

1 Press BROWN/SAUTÉ on **CROCK-POT®** Express Crock Multi-Cooker; heat 1 tablespoon oil on HIGH. Season lamb with ½ teaspoon salt and pepper. Add 2 lamb shanks; cook, uncovered, 8 to 10 minutes or until browned on all sides. Remove to large plate. Repeat with remaining oil and lamb shanks.

2 Add onion, celery, carrots, garlic and basil; cook and stir 3 to 4 minutes or until vegetables are softened. Stir in tomatoes, tomato paste and remaining ¼ teaspoon salt. Add lamb shanks to Express Crock; turn to coat. Secure lid. Press MEAT/STEW, set pressure to HIGH and time to 45 minutes. Make sure Steam Release Valve is in the "Seal" (closed) position. Press START/STOP.

3 Once cooking is complete, natural release pressure 10 minutes. Release remaining pressure. Remove lamb to large serving platter; cover to keep warm. Press BROWN/SAUTÉ on Express Crock; cook sauce, uncovered, 5 minutes or until thickened. Serve lamb with sauce. Garnish with parsley.

BRAISED LAMB SHANKS (SLOW COOK)

2 tablespoons olive oil

4 (12- to 14-ounce) lamb shanks

¾ teaspoon salt, divided

¼ teaspoon black pepper

1 medium onion, chopped

2 stalks celery, chopped

2 carrots, chopped

6 cloves garlic, minced

1 teaspoon dried basil

1 can (about 14 ounces) diced tomatoes

2 tablespoons tomato paste

Chopped fresh Italian parsley (optional)

1 Press BROWN/SAUTÉ on **CROCK-POT®** Express Crock Multi-Cooker; heat 1 tablespoon oil on HIGH. Season lamb with ½ teaspoon salt and pepper. Add 2 lamb shanks; cook, uncovered, 8 to 10 minutes or until browned on all sides. Remove to large plate. Repeat with remaining oil and lamb shanks.

2 Add onion, celery, carrots, garlic and basil; cook and stir 3 to 4 minutes or until vegetables are softened. Stir in tomatoes, tomato paste and remaining ¼ teaspoon salt; cook and stir 2 to 3 minutes or until slightly thickened. Add lamb shanks to Express Crock; turn to coat. Secure lid. Press SLOW COOK, set temperature to LOW and time to 8 to 9 hours. Make sure Steam Release Valve is in the "Release" (open) position. Press START/STOP.

3 Once cooking is complete and lamb is tender, remove lamb to large serving platter. Cover to keep warm. Press BROWN/SAUTÉ on Express Crock; cook sauce, uncovered, 5 minutes or until thickened. Serve lamb with sauce. Garnish with parsley.

ANDOUILLE AND CABBAGE (PRESSURE)

1 tablespoon olive oil

1 pound cooked andouille sausage, cut evenly into 3- to 4-inch pieces

1 medium onion, cut into ½-inch wedges

1 small head cabbage, cut evenly into 8 wedges

3 medium carrots, quartered lengthwise and cut into 3-inch pieces

8 new potatoes, cut in half

1 cup chicken broth

½ cup apple juice

1 Press BROWN/SAUTÉ on **CROCK-POT®** Express Crock Multi-Cooker; heat oil on HIGH. Add sausage; cook and stir 3 to 5 minutes or until browned. Add onion; cook and stir 3 minutes.

2 Add cabbage, carrots, potatoes, broth and apple juice to Express Crock. Secure lid. Press MEAT/STEW, set pressure to HIGH and time to 12 minutes. Make sure Steam Release Valve is in the "Seal" (closed) position. Press START/STOP.

3 Once cooking is complete, quick release pressure. Remove with slotted spoon to large serving bowl.

ANDOUILLE AND CABBAGE (SLOW COOK)

1 tablespoon olive oil

1 pound andouille sausage, cut evenly into 3- to 4-inch pieces

1 small head cabbage, cut evenly into 8 wedges

1 medium onion, cut into ½-inch wedges

3 medium carrots, quartered lengthwise and cut into 3-inch pieces

8 new potatoes, cut in half

1 can (about 14 ounces) chicken broth

½ cup apple juice

1 Press BROWN/SAUTÉ on **CROCK-POT®** Express Crock Multi-Cooker; heat oil on HIGH. Add sausage; cook and stir 3 to 5 minutes or until browned.

2 Add cabbage, onion, carrots, potatoes, broth and apple juice to Express Crock. Secure lid. Press SLOW COOK, set temperature to HIGH and time to 4 hours. Make sure Steam Release Valve is in the "Release" (open) position. Press START/STOP.

3 Once cooking is complete, remove with slotted spoon to large serving bowl.

SOUTHWEST-STYLE MEAT LOAF (PRESSURE)

2 cups water

1½ pounds ground beef

2 eggs

1 small onion, chopped (about ½ cup)

½ medium green bell pepper, chopped (about ½ cup)

½ cup plain dry bread crumbs

¾ cup chunky salsa, divided

1½ teaspoons ground cumin

¾ cup (3 ounces) shredded Mexican cheese blend

¾ teaspoon salt

¼ teaspoon black pepper

1 Place rack and water in **CROCK-POT®** Express Crock Multi-Cooker. Combine beef, eggs, onion, bell pepper, bread crumbs, ¼ cup salsa, cumin, cheese, salt and black pepper in large bowl; mix well. Shape mixture into 7×5-inch oval.

2 Tear off 18×2-inch piece of foil; fold in half crosswise to create 12×9-inch rectangle. Place meat loaf on foil; bring up sides of foil to create pan, leaving top of meat loaf uncovered. Top meat loaf with remaining ½ cup salsa. Place foil with meat loaf on rack.

3 Secure lid. Press MEAT/STEW, set pressure to HIGH and time to 42 minutes. Make sure Steam Release Valve is in the "Seal" (closed) position. Press START/STOP.

4 Once cooking is complete, quick release pressure. Remove meat loaf to large cutting board; let stand 10 minutes before slicing.

SOUTHWEST-STYLE MEAT LOAF (SLOW COOK)

2 cups water

1½ pounds ground beef

2 eggs

1 small onion, chopped (about ½ cup)

½ medium green bell pepper, chopped (about ½ cup)

½ cup plain dry bread crumbs

¾ cup chunky salsa, divided

1½ teaspoons ground cumin

¾ cup (3 ounces) shredded Mexican cheese blend

¾ teaspoon salt

¼ teaspoon black pepper

1 Place rack and water in **CROCK-POT®** Express Crock Multi-Cooker. Combine beef, eggs, onion, bell pepper, bread crumbs, ¼ cup salsa, cumin, cheese, salt and black pepper in large bowl; mix well. Shape mixture into 7×5-inch oval.

2 Tear off 18×2-inch piece of foil; fold in half crosswise to create 12×9-inch rectangle. Place meat loaf on foil; bring up sides of foil to create pan, leaving top of meat loaf uncovered. Top meat loaf with remaining ½ cup salsa. Place foil with meat loaf on rack.

3 Secure lid. Press SLOW COOK, set temperature and time to LOW 7 to 8 hours or to HIGH 3 to 4 hours. Make sure Steam Release Valve is in the "Release" (open) position. Press START/STOP.

4 Once cooking is complete, remove meat loaf to large cutting board; let stand 10 minutes before slicing.

CHAPTER 4

SIDE DISHES

CONFETTI
BLACK BEANS
(page 152)

GARLIC AND
HERB POLENTA
(page 142)

SPINACH
ARTICHOKE GRATIN
(page 160)

HARVARD BEETS
(page 132)

MUSHROOM
WILD RICE
(page 146)

CANDIED SWEET
POTATOES
(page 158)

LEMON AND TANGERINE GLAZED CARROTS (PRESSURE)

- 6 cups sliced carrots
- 1½ cups apple juice
- 6 tablespoons butter
- ¼ cup packed brown sugar
- 2 tablespoons grated lemon peel
- 2 tablespoons grated tangerine peel
- ½ teaspoon salt
- Chopped fresh Italian parsley (optional)

1 Combine carrots, apple juice, butter, brown sugar, lemon peel, tangerine peel and salt in **CROCK-POT®** Express Crock Multi-Cooker; stir to blend. Secure lid. Press STEAM, set pressure to HIGH and time to 3 minutes. Make sure Steam Release Valve is in the "Seal" (closed) position. Press START/STOP.

2 Once cooking is complete, quick release pressure. Garnish with parsley.

LEMON AND TANGERINE GLAZED CARROTS (SLOW COOK)

MAKES 10 TO 12 SERVINGS

- 6 cups sliced carrots
- 1½ cups apple juice
- 6 tablespoons butter
- ¼ cup packed brown sugar
- 2 tablespoons grated lemon peel
- 2 tablespoons grated tangerine peel
- ½ teaspoon salt
- Chopped fresh Italian parsley (optional)

1 Combine carrots, apple juice, butter, brown sugar, lemon peel, tangerine peel and salt in **CROCK-POT®** Express Crock Multi-Cooker; stir to blend. Secure lid. Press SLOW COOK, set temperature and time to LOW 4 to 5 hours or to HIGH 1 to 3 hours. Make sure Steam Release Valve is in the "Release" (open) position. Press START/STOP.

2 Once cooking is complete, garnish with parsley.

WILD RICE AND
DRIED CHERRY RISOTTO (PRESSURE)

MAKES 4 TO 6 SERVINGS

- 6 teaspoons sesame oil, divided
- 1 cup chopped onion
- 1 cup diced carrots
- 1 cup chopped green or red bell pepper
- 2 cups water
- 1⅓ cups uncooked wild rice
- 1 cup dry-roasted salted peanuts
- ½ cup dried cherries
- ¼ cup teriyaki or soy sauce
- ⅛ to ¼ teaspoon red pepper flakes
- 1 teaspoon salt

1 Press BROWN/SAUTÉ on **CROCK-POT®** Express Crock Multi-Cooker; heat 2 teaspoons oil on HIGH. Add onion, carrots and bell peppers; cook and stir 3 minutes or until vegetables are softened. Add water and rice; stir to combine. Secure lid. Press RICE/RISOTTO, set pressure to LOW and time to 25 minutes. Make sure Steam Release Valve is in the "Seal" (closed) position. Press START/STOP.

2 Once cooking is complete, natural release pressure 10 minutes. Release remaining pressure. Stir in peanuts, cherries, teriyaki sauce, red pepper flakes, salt and remaining 4 teaspoons oil.

WILD RICE AND
DRIED CHERRY RISOTTO (SLOW COOK)

MAKES 4 TO 6 SERVINGS

- 6 tablespoons sesame oil, divided
- 1 cup chopped onion
- 1 cup diced carrots
- 1 cup chopped green or red bell pepper
- 4 cups water
- 1⅓ cups uncooked wild rice
- 1 cup dry-roasted salted peanuts
- ½ cup dried cherries
- ¼ cup teriyaki or soy sauce
- ⅛ to ¼ teaspoon red pepper flakes
- 1 teaspoon salt

1 Press BROWN/SAUTÉ on **CROCK-POT®** Express Crock Multi-Cooker; heat 2 teaspoons oil on HIGH. Add onion, carrots and bell peppers; cook and stir 3 minutes or until vegetables are softened. Add water and rice; stir to combine. Secure lid. Press SLOW COOK, set temperature to HIGH and time to 3 hours. Make sure Steam Release Valve is in the "Release" (open) position. Press START/STOP.

2 Once cooking is complete, stir in peanuts, cherries, teriyaki sauce, red pepper flakes, salt and remaining 4 teaspoons oil.

BRUSSELS SPROUTS WITH BACON, THYME AND RAISINS (PRESSURE)

2 thick slices applewood smoked bacon, chopped

2 pounds Brussels sprouts, ends trimmed and cut in half lengthwise

½ cup chicken broth

⅔ cup golden raisins

2 tablespoons chopped fresh thyme

1 Press BROWN/SAUTÉ on **CROCK-POT**® Express Crock Multi-Cooker. Add bacon; cook and stir until crisp. Remove to small paper towel-lined plate using slotted spoon. Crumble and set aside. Reserve drippings.

2 Combine sprouts, broth, raisins and thyme with bacon drippings in Express Crock; stir to blend. Secure lid. Press STEAM, set pressure to HIGH and time to 5 minutes. Make sure Steam Release Valve is in the "Seal" (closed) position. Press START/STOP.

3 Once cooking is complete, quick release pressure. Top each serving with reserved bacon.

BRUSSELS SPROUTS WITH BACON, THYME AND RAISINS (SLOW COOK)

MAKES 8 SERVINGS

2 thick slices applewood smoked bacon, chopped

2 pounds Brussels sprouts, ends trimmed and cut in half lengthwise

1 cup chicken broth

⅔ cup golden raisins

2 tablespoons chopped fresh thyme

1 Press BROWN/SAUTÉ on **CROCK-POT**® Express Crock Multi-Cooker. Add bacon; cook and stir until crisp. Remove to small paper towel-lined plate using slotted spoon. Crumble and set aside. Reserve drippings.

2 Combine sprouts, broth, raisins and thyme with bacon drippings in Express Crock; stir to blend. Secure lid. Press SLOW COOK, set temperature to LOW and time to 3 to 4 hours. Make sure Steam Release Valve is in the "Release" (open) position. Press START/STOP.

3 Once cooking is complete, top each serving with reserved bacon.

GARLIC AND HERB POLENTA (PRESSURE)

2 cups corn grits

6 cups vegetable broth

2 tablespoons butter

2 teaspoons salt

2 teaspoons finely minced garlic

3 tablespoons chopped fresh herbs such as parsley, chives, thyme or chervil (or a combination)

1 Coat inside of **CROCK-POT®** Express Crock Multi-Cooker with nonstick cooking spray. Add corn grits, broth, butter, salt and garlic; stir to blend. Secure lid. Press RICE/RISOTTO, set pressure to HIGH and time to 6 minutes. Make sure Steam Release Valve is in the "Seal" (closed) position. Press START/STOP.

2 Once cooking is complete, natural release 5 minutes. Release remaining pressure. Stir in herbs just before serving.

GARLIC AND HERB POLENTA (SLOW COOK)

8 cups vegetable broth

2 cups corn grits

2 tablespoons butter

2 teaspoons finely minced garlic

2 teaspoons salt

3 tablespoons chopped fresh herbs such as parsley, chives, thyme or chervil (or a combination)

1 Coat inside of **CROCK-POT®** Express Crock Multi-Cooker with nonstick cooking spray. Add broth, corn grits, butter, garlic and salt; stir to blend. Secure lid. Press SLOW COOK, set temperature and time to LOW 4 hours or to HIGH 3 hours. Make sure Steam Release Valve is in the "Release" (open) position. Press START/STOP.

2 Once cooking is complete, stir in chopped herbs just before serving.

TIP: Polenta may also be poured into a greased 13×9-inch pan and allowed to cool until set. Cut into squares (or slice as desired) to serve. For even more great flavor, chill polenta slices until firm, then grill or fry until golden brown.

GREEN BEAN CASSEROLE (PRESSURE)

MAKES 6 SERVINGS

2 pounds fresh green beans

1 can (10¾ ounces) condensed cream of mushroom soup, undiluted

½ cup water

1 tablespoon chopped fresh Italian parsley

1 tablespoon chopped roasted red peppers

1 teaspoon dried sage

½ teaspoon salt

½ teaspoon black pepper

¼ teaspoon ground nutmeg

½ cup toasted slivered almonds*

To toast almonds, spread in single layer in Express Crock. Press BROWN/SAUTÉ. Cook and stir on HIGH heat 1 to 2 minutes or until nuts are lightly browned.

1 Combine beans, soup, water, parsley, red peppers, sage, salt, black pepper and nutmeg in **CROCK-POT®** Express Crock Multi-Cooker; stir to blend. Secure lid. Press STEAM, set pressure to HIGH and time to 3 minutes. Make sure Steam Release Valve is in the "Seal" (closed) position. Press START/STOP.

2 Once cooking is complete, quick release pressure. Sprinkle with almonds.

GREEN BEAN CASSEROLE (SLOW COOK)

MAKES 6 SERVINGS

2 pounds fresh green beans

1 can (10¾ ounces) condensed cream of mushroom soup, undiluted

1 tablespoon chopped parsley

1 tablespoon chopped roasted red peppers

1 teaspoon dried sage

½ teaspoon salt

½ teaspoon black pepper

¼ teaspoon ground nutmeg

½ cup toasted slivered almonds*

To toast almonds, spread in single layer in Express Crock. Press BROWN/SAUTÉ. Cook and stir on HIGH heat 1 to 2 minutes or until nuts are lightly browned.

1 Combine beans, soup, parsley, red peppers, sage, salt, black pepper and nutmeg in **CROCK-POT®** Express Crock Multi-Cooker; stir to blend. Secure lid. Press SLOW COOK, set temperature to LOW and time to 3 to 4 hours. Make sure Steam Release Valve is in the "Release" (open) position. Press START/STOP.

2 Once cooking is complete, sprinkle each serving evenly with almonds.

MUSHROOM WILD RICE (PRESSURE)

1 cup vegetable broth

1 cup uncooked wild rice

½ cup diced onion

½ cup sliced mushrooms

½ cup diced red or green bell pepper

Salt and black pepper

1 Combine broth, rice, onion, mushrooms, bell pepper, salt and black pepper in **CROCK-POT®** Express Crock Multi-Cooker; stir to blend. Secure lid. Press RICE/RISOTTO, set pressure to LOW and time to 12 minutes. Make sure Steam Release Valve is in the "Seal" (closed) position. Press START/STOP.

2 Once cooking is complete, natural release pressure 10 minutes. Release remaining pressure. Remove to large serving bowl.

MUSHROOM WILD RICE (SLOW COOK)

1½ cups vegetable broth

1 cup uncooked wild rice

½ cup diced onion

½ cup sliced mushrooms

½ cup diced red or green bell pepper

1 tablespoon olive oil

Salt and black pepper

1 Combine broth, rice, onion, mushrooms, bell pepper, oil, salt and black pepper in **CROCK-POT®** Express Crock Multi-Cooker; stir to blend. Secure lid. Press SLOW COOK, set temperature to HIGH and time to 2½ hours. Make sure Steam Release Valve is in the "Release" (open) position. Press START/STOP.

2 Once cooking is complete, rice is tender and liquid is absorbed, remove to large serving bowl.

RED CABBAGE AND APPLES (PRESSURE)

MAKES 6 SERVINGS

1 small head red cabbage, cored and thinly sliced

1 large apple, peeled and grated

¾ cup sugar

½ cup red wine vinegar

1 teaspoon ground cloves

Fresh apple slices (optional)

1 Combine cabbage, grated apple, sugar, vinegar and cloves in **CROCK-POT®** Express Crock Multi-Cooker; stir to blend. Secure lid. Press STEAM, set pressure to HIGH and time to 6 minutes. Make sure Steam Release Valve is in the "Seal" (closed) position. Press START/STOP.

2 Once cooking is complete, natural release pressure 10 minutes. Release remaining pressure. Garnish with apple slices.

RED CABBAGE AND APPLES (SLOW COOK)

MAKES 6 SERVINGS

1 small head red cabbage, cored and thinly sliced

1 large apple, peeled and grated

¾ cup sugar

½ cup red wine vinegar

1 teaspoon ground cloves

Fresh apple slices (optional)

1 Combine cabbage, grated apple, sugar, vinegar and cloves in **CROCK-POT®** Express Crock Multi-Cooker. Secure lid. Press SLOW COOK, set temperature to HIGH and time to 6 hours. Make sure Steam Release Valve is in the "Release" (open) position. Press START/STOP.

2 Once cooking is complete, garnish with apple slices.

FAST-COOKED POTATOES (PRESSURE)

16 small new red potatoes, unpeeled

1 cup vegetable broth

3 tablespoons butter, cubed

1 teaspoon paprika

½ teaspoon salt

¼ teaspoon garlic powder

Black pepper

1 Combine potatoes, broth, butter, paprika, salt, garlic powder and pepper in **CROCK-POT®** Express Crock Multi-Cooker; stir to blend. Secure lid. Press STEAM, set pressure to HIGH and time to 6 minutes. Make sure Steam Release Valve is in the "Seal" (closed) position. Press START/STOP.

2 Once cooking is complete, quick release pressure. Remove potatoes to large serving bowl using slotted spoon. Pour desired amount of cooking liquid over potatoes to serve.

SLOW-COOKED POTATOES (SLOW COOK)

16 small new red potatoes, unpeeled

3 tablespoons butter, cubed

1 teaspoon paprika

½ teaspoon salt

¼ teaspoon garlic powder

Black pepper

1 Combine potatoes, butter, paprika, salt, garlic powder and pepper in **CROCK-POT®** Express Crock Multi-Cooker; stir to blend. Secure lid. Press SLOW COOK, set temperature and time to LOW 7 hours or to HIGH 4 hours. Make sure Steam Release Valve is in the "Release" (open) position. Press START/STOP.

2 Once cooking is complete, remove potatoes to large serving bowl using slotted spoon. Pour desired amount of cooking liquid over potatoes to serve.

CONFETTI BLACK BEANS (PRESSURE)

2 cups vegetable broth

1 cup dried black beans, rinsed and sorted

1½ teaspoons salt, divided

1 whole bay leaf

1 tablespoon olive oil

1 medium onion, chopped

1 cup chopped bell pepper (red, yellow, green or a combination)

1 jalapeño pepper, finely chopped*

2 cloves garlic, minced

1 large tomato, chopped

½ teaspoon ground cumin

½ teaspoon chili powder

⅛ teaspoon black pepper

Jalapeño peppers can sting and irritate the skin, so wear rubber gloves when handling peppers and do not touch your eyes.

1 Combine broth, beans, 1 teaspoon salt and bay leaf in **CROCK-POT®** Express Crock Multi-Cooker. Secure lid. Press BEANS/CHILI, set pressure to HIGH and time to 23 minutes. Make sure Steam Release Valve is in the "Seal" (closed) position. Press START/STOP.

2 Once cooking is complete, quick release pressure. Drain beans. Press BROWN/SAUTÉ on Express Crock; heat oil on HIGH. Add onion, bell peppers, jalapeño pepper and garlic; cook and stir 3 minutes or until vegetables are tender. Add tomato, cumin, chili powder, remaining ½ teaspoon salt and black pepper; cook and stir 1 minute. Stir in beans; mix well. Remove and discard bay leaf. Remove to large serving bowl.

CONFETTI BLACK BEANS (SLOW COOK)

1 cup dried black beans, rinsed and sorted

1½ teaspoons olive oil

1 medium onion, chopped

¼ cup chopped red bell pepper

¼ cup chopped yellow bell pepper

1 jalapeño pepper, finely chopped*

2 cloves garlic, minced

1 large tomato, chopped

½ teaspoon ground cumin

½ teaspoon chili powder

1 teaspoon salt

⅛ teaspoon black pepper

1 can (about 14 ounces) chicken broth

1 whole bay leaf

Jalapeño peppers can sting and irritate the skin, so wear rubber gloves when handling peppers and do not touch your eyes.

1 Place beans in large bowl and add enough cold water to cover by at least 2 inches. Soak 6 to 8 hours or overnight.** Drain beans; discard water.

2 Press BROWN/SAUTÉ on **CROCK-POT®** Express Crock Multi-Cooker; heat oil on HIGH. Add onion, bell peppers, jalapeño pepper and garlic; cook and stir 3 minutes or until vegetables are tender. Add tomato, cumin, chili powder, salt and black pepper; cook and stir 1 minute. Add beans, broth and bay leaf to Express Crock. Secure lid. Press SLOW COOK, set temperature to LOW 7 to 8 hours or to HIGH 4½ to 5 hours. Make sure Steam Release Valve is in the "Release" (open) position. Press START/STOP.

3 Once cooking is complete, remove and discard bay leaf. Remove to large serving bowl.

**To quick soak beans, place beans in large saucepan; cover with water. Bring to a boil over high heat. Boil 2 minutes. Remove from heat; let soak, covered, 1 hour.

BARLEY RISOTTO WITH FENNEL (PRESSURE)

- 2 tablespoons oil
- 1 medium fennel bulb, cored and finely diced (about ½ cup)
- 1 shallot, finely chopped
- 1 clove garlic, minced
- 3 cups vegetable broth
- 1½ cups frozen cut green beans
- 1 cup uncooked pearl barley
- 1 carrot, finely chopped
- 1 teaspoon ground fennel seed
- ½ cup grated Parmesan cheese
- 1 tablespoon grated lemon peel
- 1 teaspoon black pepper

1 Press BROWN/SAUTÉ on **CROCK-POT®** Express Crock Multi-Cooker; heat oil on HIGH. Add fennel, shallot and garlic; cook and stir 3 minutes. Stir in broth, beans, barley, carrot and fennel seed. Secure lid. Press RICE/RISOTTO, set pressure to HIGH and time to 20 minutes. Make sure Steam Release Valve is in the "Seal" (closed) position. Press START/STOP.

2 Once cooking is complete, natural release pressure 10 minutes. Release remaining pressure. Stir in cheese, lemon peel and pepper.

BARLEY RISOTTO WITH FENNEL (SLOW COOK)

- 2 tablespoons oil
- 1 medium fennel bulb, cored and finely diced (about ½ cup)
- 1 shallot, finely chopped
- 1 clove garlic, minced
- 3 cups vegetable broth
- 1½ cups frozen cut green beans
- 1 cup uncooked pearl barley
- 1 carrot, finely chopped
- 2 teaspoons ground fennel seed
- ½ cup grated Parmesan cheese
- 1 tablespoon grated lemon peel
- 1 teaspoon black pepper

1 Press BROWN/SAUTÉ on **CROCK-POT®** Express Crock Multi-Cooker; heat oil on HIGH. Add fennel, shallot and garlic; cook and stir 3 minutes. Stir in broth, beans, barley, carrot and fennel seed. Secure lid. Press SLOW COOK, set temperature to HIGH and time to 3 hours. Make sure Steam Release Valve is in the "Release" (open) position. Press START/STOP.

2 Once cooking is complete and barley is thick and creamy, stir in cheese, lemon peel and pepper.

FAST-COOKED SUCCOTASH (PRESSURE)

MAKES 8 SERVINGS

2 teaspoons olive oil

1 cup diced onion

1 cup diced green bell pepper

1 cup diced celery

1 can (about 14 ounces) diced tomatoes

1½ cups frozen corn

1½ cups frozen lima beans

1 tablespoon minced fresh Italian parsley

1 teaspoon paprika

Salt and black pepper

1 Press BROWN/SAUTÉ on **CROCK-POT®** Express Crock Multi-Cooker; heat oil on HIGH. Add onion, bell pepper and celery; cook and stir 5 minutes or until vegetables are tender. Stir in tomatoes, corn, beans, parsley, paprika, salt and black pepper. Secure lid. Press BEANS/CHILI, set pressure to HIGH and time to 3 minutes. Make sure Steam Release Valve is in the "Seal" (closed) position. Press START/STOP.

2 Once cooking is complete, quick release pressure. Remove to large serving bowl.

SLOW-COOKED SUCCOTASH (SLOW COOK)

MAKES 8 SERVINGS

2 teaspoons olive oil

1 cup diced onion

1 cup diced green bell pepper

1 cup diced celery

1 teaspoon paprika

1½ cups frozen corn

1½ cups frozen lima beans

1 cup canned diced tomatoes

1 tablespoon minced fresh Italian parsley

Salt and black pepper

1 Press BROWN/SAUTÉ on **CROCK-POT®** Express Crock Multi-Cooker; heat oil on HIGH. Add onion, bell pepper and celery; cook and stir 5 minutes or until vegetables are tender. Stir in paprika.

2 Stir onion mixture, corn, beans, tomatoes, parsley, salt and black pepper into Express Crock. Secure lid. Press SLOW COOK, set temperature and time to LOW 6 to 8 hours or to HIGH 3 to 4 hours. Make sure Steam Release Valve is in the "Release" (open) position. Press START/STOP.

3 Once cooking is complete, remove to large serving bowl.

CANDIED SWEET POTATOES (PRESSURE)

3 medium sweet potatoes (1½ to 2 pounds), peeled and sliced into ½-inch rounds

1 cup water

¼ cup (½ stick) butter, cut into small pieces

2 tablespoons sugar

1 tablespoon vanilla

1 teaspoon ground nutmeg

1 Combine potatoes, water, butter, sugar, vanilla and nutmeg in **CROCK-POT®** Express Crock Multi-Cooker. Secure lid. Press STEAM, set pressure to HIGH and time to 5 minutes. Make sure Steam Release Valve is in the "Seal" (closed) position. Press START/STOP.

2 Once cooking is complete, quick release pressure. Remove potatoes to large serving bowl using slotted spoon.

CANDIED SWEET POTATOES (SLOW COOK)

MAKES 4 SERVINGS

3 medium sweet potatoes (1½ to 2 pounds), peeled and sliced into ½-inch rounds

½ cup water

¼ cup (½ stick) butter, cut into small pieces

2 tablespoons sugar

1 tablespoon vanilla

1 teaspoon ground nutmeg

1 Combine potatoes, water, butter, sugar, vanilla and nutmeg in **CROCK-POT®** Express Crock Multi-Cooker. Secure lid. Press SLOW COOK, set temperature and time to LOW 7 hours or to HIGH 4 hours. Make sure Steam Release Valve is in the "Release" (open) position. Press START/STOP.

2 Once cooking is complete, remove potatoes to large serving bowl using slotted spoon.

SPINACH ARTICHOKE GRATIN (PRESSURE)

1½ cups water

2 cups (16 ounces) cottage cheese

2 eggs

4½ tablespoons grated Parmesan cheese, divided

1 tablespoon lemon juice

⅛ teaspoon ground nutmeg

⅛ teaspoon black pepper

2 cups chopped fresh spinach

⅓ cup thinly sliced green onions

1 can (14 ounces) artichoke hearts, drained

1 Spray 6- to 7-inch (1½-quart) soufflé dish or round baking dish that fits inside of **CROCK-POT®** Express Crock Multi-Cooker with nonstick cooking spray. Prepare foil handles (page 13). Place rack in Express Crock; add water.

2 Add cottage cheese, eggs, 3 tablespoons Parmesan cheese, lemon juice, nutmeg and pepper to food processor or blender; process until smooth. Combine cottage cheese mixture, spinach and green onions in large bowl; stir to blend.

3 Spread half of cottage cheese mixture in prepared dish. Pat artichoke halves dry with paper towels. Place in single layer over spinach mixture. Sprinkle with remaining 1½ tablespoons Parmesan cheese; top with remaining cottage cheese mixture. Cover dish with foil; place on rack in Express Crock using foil handles. Secure lid. Press STEAM, set pressure to HIGH and time to 10 minutes. Make sure Steam Release Valve is in the "Seal" (closed) position. Press START/STOP.

4 Once cooking is complete, quick release pressure. Remove dish from Express Crock using foil handles.

SPINACH ARTICHOKE GRATIN (SLOW COOK)

1½ cups water

2 cups (16 ounces) cottage cheese

2 eggs

4½ tablespoons grated Parmesan cheese, divided

1 tablespoon lemon juice

⅛ teaspoon ground nutmeg

⅛ teaspoon black pepper

2 cups chopped fresh spinach

⅓ cup thinly sliced green onions

1 can (14 ounces) artichoke hearts, drained

1 Spray 6- to 7-inch (1½-quart) soufflé dish or round baking dish that fits inside of **CROCK-POT®** Express Crock Multi-Cooker with nonstick cooking spray. Prepare foil handles (page 13). Place rack in Express Crock; add water.

2 Add cottage cheese, eggs, 3 tablespoons Parmesan cheese, lemon juice, nutmeg and pepper to food processor or blender; process until smooth. Combine cottage cheese mixture, spinach and green onions in large bowl; stir to blend.

3 Spread half of cottage cheese mixture in prepared dish. Pat artichoke halves dry with paper towels. Place in single layer over spinach mixture. Sprinkle with remaining 1½ tablespoons Parmesan cheese; top with remaining cottage cheese mixture. Cover dish with foil; place on rack in Express Crock using foil handles. Secure lid. Press SLOW COOK, set temperature and time to LOW 3 to 3½ hours or to HIGH 2 to 2½ hours. Make sure Steam Release Valve is in the "Release" (open) position. Press START/STOP.

4 Once cooking is complete, remove dish from Express Crock using foil handles.

CHAPTER 5

DESSERTS

VANILLA SOUR
CREAM CHEESECAKE
(page 180)

BROWNIE
BOTTOMS
(page 168)

CHERRY DELIGHT
(page 174)

CINNAMON-GINGER
POACHED PEARS
(page 166)

PINEAPPLE
RICE PUDDING
(page 182)

CHOCOLATE CHIP
BREAD PUDDING
(page 176)

ENGLISH BREAD PUDDING (PRESSURE)

1½ cups water

8 ounces stale bread, cut into 1-inch pieces

1 cup chopped apple

¾ cup mixed dried fruit (raisins, cranberries, dates, etc.)

¼ cup chopped nuts

1¾ cups milk

2 eggs

¼ cup packed brown sugar

2 tablespoons butter, melted

½ teaspoon ground cinnamon

⅛ teaspoon ground nutmeg

Pinch ground cloves

Pinch salt

Apple slices (optional)

1 Spray 6- to 7-inch (1½-quart) soufflé dish or round baking dish that fits inside **CROCK-POT®** Express Crock Multi-Cooker with nonstick cooking spray. Prepare foil handles (page 13). Place rack in Express Crock; add water.

2 Combine bread, chopped apples, dried fruit and nuts in medium bowl. Whisk milk, eggs, brown sugar, butter, cinnamon, nutmeg, cloves and salt in another medium bowl. Pour over bread mixture; stir to coat. Let stand 15 minutes, stirring occasionally.

3 Remove bread mixture to prepared dish; cover with foil. Place dish on rack using foil handles. Press DESSERT, set pressure to HIGH and time to 45 minutes. Make sure Steam Release Valve is in the "Seal" (closed) position. Press START/STOP.

4 Once cooking is complete, use natural release 10 minutes. Release remaining pressure. Garnish each serving with apple slices.

ENGLISH BREAD PUDDING (SLOW COOK)

1½ cups water

8 ounces stale bread, cut into 1-inch pieces

1 cup chopped apple

¾ cup mixed dried fruit (raisins, cranberries, dates, etc.)

¼ cup chopped nuts

1¼ cups milk

2 eggs

¼ cup packed brown sugar

2 tablespoons butter, melted

½ teaspoon ground cinnamon

⅛ teaspoon ground nutmeg

Pinch ground cloves

Pinch salt

Apple slices (optional)

1 Spray 6- to 7-inch (1½-quart) soufflé dish or round baking dish that fits inside **CROCK-POT®** Express Crock Multi-Cooker with nonstick cooking spray. Prepare foil handles (page 13). Place rack in Express Crock; add water.

2 Combine bread, chopped apples, dried fruit and nuts in medium bowl. Whisk milk, eggs, brown sugar, butter, cinnamon, nutmeg, cloves and salt in another medium bowl. Pour over bread mixture; stir to coat. Let stand 15 minutes, stirring occasionally.

3 Remove bread mixture to prepared dish; cover with foil. Place dish on rack using foil handles. Secure lid. Press SLOW COOK, set temperature to LOW and time to 3½ to 4 hours. Make sure Steam Release Valve is in the "Release" (open) position. Press START/STOP.

4 Once cooking is complete and toothpick inserted into center of pudding comes out clean, garnish with apple slices.

CINNAMON-GINGER POACHED PEARS (PRESSURE)

3 cups water	10 slices fresh ginger, ¼ inch thick	1 tablespoon chopped candied ginger
1 cup sugar	2 whole cinnamon sticks	6 Bosc or Anjou pears, peeled and cored

1 Combine water, sugar, ginger, cinnamon and candied ginger in **CROCK-POT®** Express Crock Multi-Cooker. Add rack; place pears on top. Secure lid. Press STEAM, set pressure to LOW and time to 3 minutes. Make sure Steam Release Valve is in the "Seal" (closed) position. Press START/STOP.

2 Once cooking is complete, quick release pressure. Remove pears to large serving platter. Press BROWN/SAUTÉ on Express Crock; cook syrup, uncovered, on HIGH 10 minutes or until thickened. Remove and discard cinnamon sticks. Serve pears with syrup.

CINNAMON-GINGER POACHED PEARS (SLOW COOK)

MAKES 6 SERVINGS

3 cups water	10 slices fresh ginger, ¼ inch thick	1 tablespoon chopped candied ginger
1 cup sugar	2 whole cinnamon sticks	6 Bosc or Anjou pears, peeled and cored

1 Combine water, sugar, ginger, cinnamon and candied ginger in **CROCK-POT®** Express Crock Multi-Cooker. Add rack; place pears on top. Secure lid. Press SLOW COOK, set temperature and time to LOW 4 to 6 hours or to HIGH 1½ to 2 hours. Make sure Steam Release Valve is in the "Release" (open) position. Press START/STOP.

2 Once cooking is complete, remove pears to large serving platter. Press BROWN/SAUTÉ on Express Crock; cook syrup, uncovered, on HIGH 10 minutes or until thickened. Remove and discard cinnamon sticks. Serve pears with syrup.

BROWNIE BOTTOMS (PRESSURE)

2 cups water, divided

2½ cups packaged brownie mix

1 package (2¾ ounces) instant chocolate pudding mix

½ cup milk chocolate chips

2 eggs, beaten

3 tablespoons butter, melted

½ cup packed brown sugar

2 tablespoons unsweetened cocoa powder

Whipped cream or ice cream (optional)

1 Spray 6- or 7-inch (1½-quart) soufflé dish or round baking dish that fits inside of **CROCK-POT®** Express Crock Multi-Cooker with nonstick cooking spray. Prepare foil handles (page 13). Place rack in Express Crock; add 1½ cups water.

2 Combine brownie mix, pudding mix, chocolate chips, eggs and butter in large bowl; stir until well blended. Combine brown sugar, remaining ½ cup water and cocoa in medium microwavable bowl. Microwave on HIGH 1 minute. Pour boiling sugar mixture over batter. Cover dish with foil; place in Express Crock using foil handles. Secure lid. Press DESSERT, set pressure to HIGH and time to 30 minutes. Make sure Steam Release Valve is in the "Seal" (closed) position. Press START/STOP.

3 Once cooking is complete, quick release pressure. Remove dish using foil handles. Let stand 10 minutes. Serve with whipped cream, if desired.

BROWNIE BOTTOMS (SLOW COOK)

MAKES 6 SERVINGS

2 cups water, divided

2½ cups packaged brownie mix

1 package (2¾ ounces) instant chocolate pudding mix

½ cup milk chocolate chips

2 eggs, beaten

3 tablespoons butter, melted

½ cup packed brown sugar

2 tablespoons unsweetened cocoa powder

Whipped cream or ice cream (optional)

1 Spray 6- or 7-inch (1½-quart) soufflé dish or round baking dish that fits inside of **CROCK-POT®** Express Crock Multi-Cooker with nonstick cooking spray. Prepare foil handles (page 13). Place rack in Express Crock; add 1½ cups water.

2 Combine brownie mix, pudding mix, chocolate chips, eggs and butter in large bowl; stir until well blended. Combine brown sugar, remaining ½ cup water and cocoa in medium microwavable bowl. Microwave on HIGH 1 minute. Pour boiling sugar mixture over batter. Cover dish with foil; place in Express Crock using foil handles. Secure lid. Press SLOW COOK, set temperature to HIGH and time to 1½ hours. Make sure Steam Release Valve is in the "Release" (open) position. Press START/STOP.

3 Once cooking is complete, remove dish using foil handles. Let stand 10 minutes. Serve with whipped cream, if desired.

CRAN-CHERRY BREAD PUDDING (PRESSURE)

1½ cups water

¾ cup whipping cream

2 egg yolks, beaten

3 tablespoons sugar

⅛ teaspoon kosher salt

¾ teaspoon cherry extract

⅓ cup dried sweetened cranberries

⅓ cup golden raisins

¼ cup whole candied red cherries, halved

¼ cup dry sherry

3 cups unseasoned stuffing mix

½ cup white chocolate baking chips

Whipped cream (optional)

1 Spray 6- to 7-inch (1½-quart) soufflé dish or round baking dish that fits inside of **CROCK-POT®** Express Crock Multi-Cooker with nonstick cooking spray. Prepare foil handles (page 13). Place rack in Express Crock; add water.

2 Press BROWN/SAUTÉ on Express Crock. Add cream, egg yolks, sugar and salt; cook and stir on HIGH 5 minutes or until mixture coats back of spoon. Remove Express Crock to large bowl of ice water; stir to cool. Stir in cherry extract. Remove to separate large bowl; press plastic wrap onto surface of custard. Refrigerate.

3 Combine cranberries, raisins and cherries in small bowl. Press BROWN/SAUTÉ on Express Crock; heat sherry on HIGH until warm. Pour over fruit; let stand 10 minutes. Wipe Express Crock clean.

4 Fold stuffing mix and baking chips into custard. Drain fruit, reserving sherry; stir into custard. Pour into prepared dish. Top with reserved sherry; cover tightly with foil. Place prepared dish on rack using foil handles. Secure lid. Press DESSERT, set pressure to HIGH and time to 45 minutes. Make sure Steam Release Valve is in the "Seal" (closed) position. Press START/STOP.

5 Once cooking is complete, natural release pressure 10 minutes. Release remaining pressure. Remove dish using foil handles. Uncover; let stand 10 minutes. Serve warm with whipped cream, if desired.

CRAN-CHERRY BREAD PUDDING (SLOW COOK)

1½ cups water

¼ cup whipping cream

2 egg yolks, beaten

3 tablespoons sugar

⅛ teaspoon kosher salt

¾ teaspoon cherry extract

⅓ cup dried sweetened cranberries

⅓ cup golden raisins

¼ cup whole candied red cherries, halved

¼ cup dry sherry

3 cups unseasoned stuffing mix

½ cup white chocolate baking chips

Whipped cream (optional)

1. Spray 6- to 7-inch (1½-quart) soufflé dish or round baking dish that fits inside of **CROCK-POT®** Express Crock Multi-Cooker with nonstick cooking spray. Prepare foil handles (page 13). Place rack in Express Crock; add water.

2. Press BROWN/SAUTÉ on Express Crock. Add cream, egg yolks, sugar and salt; cook and stir on HIGH 5 minutes or until mixture coats back of spoon. Remove Express Crock to large bowl of ice water; stir to cool. Stir in cherry extract. Remove to separate large bowl; press plastic wrap onto surface of custard. Refrigerate.

3. Combine cranberries, raisins and cherries in small bowl. Press BROWN/SAUTÉ on Express Crock; heat sherry on HIGH until warm. Pour over fruit; let stand 10 minutes. Wipe Express Crock clean.

4. Fold stuffing mix and baking chips into custard. Drain fruit, reserving sherry; stir into custard. Pour into prepared dish. Top with reserved sherry; cover tightly with foil. Place prepared dish on rack using foil handles. Secure lid. Press SLOW COOK, set temperature to LOW and time to 4 to 5 hours. Make sure Steam Release Valve is in the "Release" (open) position. Press START/STOP.

5. Once cooking is complete and pudding springs back when touched, remove dish using foil handles. Uncover; let stand 10 minutes. Serve warm with whipped cream, if desired.

PUMPKIN CUSTARD (PRESSURE)

2 cups water

1 cup canned solid-pack pumpkin

½ cup packed brown sugar

2 eggs, beaten

½ teaspoon ground ginger

½ teaspoon grated lemon peel

½ teaspoon ground cinnamon, plus additional for garnish

1 can (12 ounces) evaporated milk

1 Place rack in **CROCK-POT®** Express Crock Multi-Cooker; add water.

2 Combine pumpkin, brown sugar, eggs, ginger, lemon peel and ½ teaspoon cinnamon in large bowl; stir in evaporated milk. Divide mixture among six (6-ounce) ramekins or custard cups. Cover each cup tightly with foil. Stack ramekins on rack. Secure lid. Press STEAM, set pressure to LOW and time to 10 minutes. Make sure Steam Release Valve is in the "Seal" (closed) position. Press START/STOP.

3 Once cooking is complete, natural release pressure 10 minutes. Release remaining pressure. Use rubber-tipped tongs or slotted spoon to remove ramekins from Express Crock. Sprinkle with additional ground cinnamon. Serve warm.

PUMPKIN CUSTARD (SLOW COOK)

MAKES 6 SERVINGS

1 cup canned solid-pack pumpkin

½ cup packed brown sugar

2 eggs, beaten

½ teaspoon ground ginger

½ teaspoon grated lemon peel

½ teaspoon ground cinnamon, plus additional for garnish

1 can (12 ounces) evaporated milk

2 cups water

1 Place rack in **CROCK-POT®** Express Crock Multi-Cooker; add water.

2 Combine pumpkin, brown sugar, eggs, ginger, lemon peel and ½ teaspoon cinnamon in large bowl; stir in evaporated milk. Divide mixture among six (6-ounce) ramekins or custard cups. Cover each cup tightly with foil. Stack ramekins on rack. Secure lid. Press SLOW COOK, set temperature to LOW and time to 4 hours. Make sure Steam Release Valve is in the "Release" (open) position. Press START/STOP.

3 Once cooking is complete, use rubber-tipped tongs or slotted spoon to remove ramekins from Express Crock. Sprinkle with additional ground cinnamon. Serve warm.

VARIATION: To make Pumpkin Custard in a single dish, pour custard into 1½-quart soufflé dish instead of ramekins. Cover and cook as directed above.

CHERRY DELIGHT (PRESSURE)

1½ cups water

1 can (21 ounces) cherry
   pie filling

1 package (about
   18 ounces) yellow
   cake mix

½ cup (1 stick) butter,
   melted

⅓ cup chopped walnuts

1 Spray 6- to 7-inch (1½-quart) soufflé dish or round baking dish that fits inside of **CROCK-POT®** Express Crock Multi-Cooker with nonstick cooking spray. Prepare foil handles (page 13). Place rack in Express Crock; add water.

2 Add pie filling to prepared dish. Combine cake mix and butter in medium bowl; spread evenly over pie filling. Cover dish with foil. Place prepared dish in Express Crock using foil handles. Secure lid. Press DESSERT, set pressure to LOW and time to 10 minutes. Make sure Steam Release Valve is in the "Seal" (closed) position. Press START/STOP.

3 Once cooking is complete, quick release pressure. Remove dish using foil handles. Sprinkle with walnuts.

CHERRY DELIGHT (SLOW COOK)

MAKES 8 TO 10 SERVINGS

1½ cups water

1 can (21 ounces) cherry
   pie filling

1 package (about
   18 ounces) yellow
   cake mix

½ cup (1 stick) butter,
   melted

⅓ cup chopped walnuts

1 Spray 6- to 7-inch (1½-quart) soufflé dish or round baking dish that fits inside of **CROCK-POT®** Express Crock Multi-Cooker with nonstick cooking spray. Prepare foil handles (page 13). Place rack in Express Crock; add water.

2 Add pie filling to prepared dish. Combine cake mix and butter in medium bowl; spread evenly over pie filling. Cover dish with foil. Place prepared dish in Express Crock using foil handles. Secure lid. Press SLOW COOK, set temperature and time to LOW 3 to 4 hours or to HIGH 1½ to 2 hours. Make sure Steam Release Valve is in the "Release" (open) position. Press START/STOP.

3 Once cooking is complete, remove dish using foil handles. Sprinkle with walnuts.

CHOCOLATE CHIP
BREAD PUDDING (PRESSURE)

Butter, softened

1½ cups water

3 slices (¾-inch-thick) day-old challah*

¼ cup semisweet chocolate chips

3 eggs

1½ cups half-and-half

⅓ cup granulated sugar

½ teaspoon vanilla

⅛ teaspoon salt

Powdered sugar

Fresh fruit (optional)

Challah is usually braided. If you use brioche or another rich egg bread, slice bread to fit baking dish.

1 Butter 6- or 7-inch (1½-quart) soufflé dish or round baking dish that fits inside of **CROCK-POT®** Express Crock Multi-Cooker. Prepare foil handles (page 13). Place rack in Express Crock; add water.

2 Arrange 1½ bread slices in bottom of dish. Sprinkle with 2 tablespoons chocolate chips. Repeat layers with remaining bread and chocolate chips. Beat eggs in medium bowl. Add half-and-half, granulated sugar, vanilla and salt; stir to blend. Pour egg mixture over bread layers. Press bread into liquid. Set aside 10 minutes or until liquid is absorbed. Cover dish with buttered foil, buttered side down.

3 Place prepared dish on rack using foil handles. Secure lid. Press DESSERT, set pressure to HIGH and time to 45 minutes. Make sure Steam Release Valve is in the "Seal" (closed) position. Press START/STOP.

4 Once cooking is complete, natural release pressure 10 minutes. Release remaining pressure. Remove dish using foil handles; let stand 10 minutes. Sprinkle with powdered sugar. Garnish with fruit.

CHOCOLATE CHIP
BREAD PUDDING (SLOW COOK)

Butter, softened

1½ cups water

3 slices (¾-inch-thick) day-old challah*

¼ cup semisweet chocolate chips

3 eggs

1½ cups half-and-half

⅓ cup granulated sugar

½ teaspoon vanilla

⅛ teaspoon salt

Powdered sugar

Fresh fruit (optional)

Challah is usually braided. If you use brioche or another rich egg bread, slice bread to fit baking dish.

1 Butter 6- or 7-inch (1½-quart) soufflé dish or round baking dish that fits inside of **CROCK-POT®** Express Crock Multi-Cooker. Prepare foil handles (page 13). Place rack in Express Crock; add water.

2 Arrange 1½ bread slices in bottom of dish. Sprinkle with 2 tablespoons chocolate chips. Repeat layers with remaining bread and chocolate chips. Beat eggs in medium bowl. Add half-and-half, granulated sugar, vanilla and salt; stir to blend. Pour egg mixture over bread layers. Press bread into liquid. Set aside 10 minutes or until liquid is absorbed. Cover dish with buttered foil, buttered side down.

3 Place prepared dish on rack using foil handles. Secure lid. Press SLOW COOK, set temperature to HIGH and time to 3 hours. Make sure Steam Release Valve is in the "Release" (open) position. Press START/STOP.

4 Once cooking is complete, remove dish using foil handles. Let stand 10 minutes. Sprinkle with powdered sugar. Garnish with fruit.

FIGS POACHED IN RED WINE (PRESSURE)

1 cup dry red wine

1 cup packed brown sugar

12 dried Calimyrna or Mediterranean figs (about 6 ounces)

2 (3-inch) whole cinnamon sticks

1 teaspoon finely grated orange peel

4 tablespoons whipping cream (optional)

1 Combine wine, brown sugar, figs, cinnamon sticks and orange peel in **CROCK-POT®** Express Crock Multi-Cooker; stir to blend. Secure lid. Press STEAM, set pressure to HIGH and time to 5 minutes. Make sure Steam Release Valve is in the "Seal" (closed) position. Press START/STOP.

2 Once cooking is complete, quick release pressure. Remove and discard cinnamon sticks. Remove figs to medium bowl using slotted spoon. Press BROWN/SAUTÉ on Express Crock; cook syrup, uncovered, on HIGH 5 minutes or until reduced by half. Spoon syrup and cream, if desired, into serving dishes; top with figs.

FIGS POACHED IN RED WINE (SLOW COOK)

1 cup dry red wine

1 cup packed brown sugar

12 dried Calimyrna or Mediterranean figs (about 6 ounces)

2 (3-inch) whole cinnamon sticks

1 teaspoon finely grated orange peel

4 tablespoons whipping cream (optional)

1 Combine wine, brown sugar, figs, cinnamon sticks and orange peel in **CROCK-POT®** Express Crock Multi-Cooker; stir to blend. Secure lid. Press SLOW COOK, set temperature and time to LOW 5 to 6 hours or to HIGH 4 to 5 hours. Make sure Steam Release Valve is in the "Release" (open) position. Press START/STOP.

2 Once cooking is complete, remove and discard cinnamon sticks. Remove figs to medium bowl using slotted spoon. Press BROWN/SAUTÉ on Express Crock; cook syrup, uncovered, on HIGH 5 minutes or until reduced by half. Spoon syrup and cream, if desired, into serving dishes; top with figs.

VANILLA SOUR CREAM CHEESECAKE
(PRESSURE)

1½ cups water

¾ cup graham cracker crumbs

¼ cup plus 3 tablespoons sugar, divided

¼ teaspoon ground nutmeg

2 tablespoons unsalted butter, melted

1 package (8 ounces) cream cheese, softened

2 eggs

¼ cup sour cream

1½ teaspoons vanilla

1½ tablespoons all-purpose flour

Fresh strawberries, sliced (optional)

Sprigs fresh mint (optional)

1 Cut parchment paper to fit bottom of 7-inch springform pan that fits inside of **CROCK-POT®** Express Crock Multi-Cooker. Lightly spray bottom and side of pan with nonstick cooking spray. Wrap bottom and side of pan with foil. Prepare foil handles (page 13). Place rack in Express Crock; add water.

2 Combine graham cracker crumbs, 1 tablespoon sugar and nutmeg in medium bowl; stir to blend. Stir in butter until well blended. Press mixture into bottom and 1 inch up sides of prepared pan. Freeze 10 minutes.

3 Meanwhile, beat cream cheese in large bowl with electric mixer at high speed 3 to 4 minutes or until smooth. Add remaining ¼ cup plus 2 tablespoons sugar; beat 1 to 2 minutes. Beat in eggs, sour cream and vanilla until blended. Stir in flour. Pour batter into crust.

4 Cover pan tightly with foil. Place prepared pan on rack using foil handles. Secure lid. Press DESSERT, set pressure to HIGH and time to 40 minutes. Make sure Steam Release Valve is in the "Seal" (closed) position. Press START/STOP.

5 Once cooking is complete, quick release pressure. Remove dish from Express Crock using foil handles. Remove foil; cool 1 hour. Run thin knife around edge of cheesecake to loosen (do not remove side of pan). Refrigerate 2 to 3 hours or overnight.

6 Remove side and bottom on pan; remove cheesecake to serving plate. Top with strawberries, if desired. Garnish with mint. Cut into wedges to serve.

VANILLA SOUR CREAM CHEESECAKE
(SLOW COOK)

1½ cups water

¾ cup graham cracker crumbs

¼ cup plus 3 tablespoons sugar, divided

¼ teaspoon ground nutmeg

2 tablespoons unsalted butter, melted

1 package (8 ounces) cream cheese, softened

2 eggs

¼ cup sour cream

1½ teaspoons vanilla

1½ tablespoons all-purpose flour

Fresh strawberries, sliced (optional)

Sprigs fresh mint (optional)

1. Cut parchment paper to fit bottom of 7-inch springform pan that fits inside of **CROCK-POT®** Express Crock Multi-Cooker. Lightly spray bottom and side of pan with nonstick cooking spray. Wrap bottom and side of pan with foil. Prepare foil handles (page 13). Place rack in Express Crock; add water.

2. Combine graham cracker crumbs, 1 tablespoon sugar and nutmeg in medium bowl; stir to blend. Stir in butter until well blended. Press mixture into bottom and 1 inch up sides of prepared pan. Freeze 10 minutes.

3. Meanwhile, beat cream cheese in large bowl with electric mixer at high speed 3 to 4 minutes or until smooth. Add remaining ¼ cup plus 2 tablespoons sugar; beat 1 to 2 minutes. Beat in eggs, sour cream and vanilla until blended. Stir in flour. Pour batter into crust.

4. Cover pan tightly with foil. Place prepared pan on rack. Secure lid. Press SLOW COOK, set temperature to HIGH and time to 2 hours. Make sure Steam Release Valve is in the "Release" (open) position. Press START/STOP.

5. Once cooking is complete, remove pan from Express Crock using foil handles. Remove foil; cool 1 hour. Run thin knife around edge of cheesecake to loosen (do not remove side of pan). Refrigerate 2 to 3 hours or overnight.

6. Remove side and bottom on pan; remove cheesecake to serving plate. Top with strawberries, if desired. Garnish with mint. Cut into wedges to serve.

PINEAPPLE RICE PUDDING (PRESSURE)

1½ cups water

¾ cup uncooked Arborio rice

¼ teaspoon salt

1 can (20 ounces) crushed pineapple in juice, undrained

1 can (13½ ounces) unsweetened coconut milk

1 can (12 ounces) evaporated milk

2 eggs, lightly beaten

¼ cup granulated sugar

¼ cup packed brown sugar

½ teaspoon ground cinnamon

¼ teaspoon ground nutmeg

Toasted coconut (optional)*

Pineapple slices (optional)

To toast coconut, spread in single layer in Express Crock. Press BROWN/SAUTÉ. Cook and stir on HIGH 1 to 2 minutes or until lightly browned. Remove from Express Crock immediately.

1 Combine water, rice and salt in **CROCK-POT®** Express Crock Multi-Cooker; stir to blend. Secure lid. Press RICE/RISOTTO, set pressure to HIGH and time to 6 minutes. Make sure Steam Release Valve is in the "Seal" (closed) position. Press START/STOP.

2 Once cooking is complete, natural release pressure 10 minutes. Release remaining pressure. Combine crushed pineapple, coconut milk, evaporated milk, eggs, sugars, cinnamon and nutmeg in large bowl; stir to blend. Stir pineapple mixture into cooked rice. Press BROWN/SAUTÉ on Express Crock; cook on HIGH 13 to 15 minutes or until thickened. Remove immediately to serving dish(es). Garnish with toasted coconut and pineapple slices.

PINEAPPLE RICE PUDDING (SLOW COOK)

1½ cups water

¼ cup uncooked Arborio rice

¼ teaspoon salt

1 can (20 ounces) crushed pineapple in juice, undrained

1 can (13½ ounces) unsweetened coconut milk

1 can (12 ounces) evaporated milk

2 eggs, lightly beaten

¼ cup granulated sugar

¼ cup packed brown sugar

½ teaspoon ground cinnamon

¼ teaspoon ground nutmeg

Toasted coconut and pineapple slices (optional)*

Pineapple slices (optional)

To toast coconut, spread in single layer in Express Crock. Press BROWN/SAUTÉ. Cook and stir on HIGH 1 to 2 minutes or until lightly browned. Remove from Express Crock immediately.

1 Combine water, rice and salt in **CROCK-POT®** Express Crock Multi-Cooker; stir to blend. Secure lid. Press SLOW COOK, set temperature to HIGH and time to 3 to 4 hours. Make sure Steam Release Valve is in the "Release" (open) position. Press START/STOP.

2 Once cooking is complete and rice is tender, combine pineapple, coconut milk, evaporated milk, eggs, sugars, cinnamon and nutmeg in large bowl; stir to blend. Stir pineapple mixture into cooked rice. Press BROWN/SAUTÉ on Express Crock; cook, uncovered, on HIGH 13 to 15 minutes or until thickened. Remove immediately to serving dish(es). Garnish with toasted coconut and pineapple slices.

TEQUILA-POACHED PEARS (PRESSURE)

2 cups water

1 can (11½ ounces) pear nectar

1 cup tequila

½ cup sugar

Grated peel and juice of 1 lime

4 Anjou pears, peeled

1 Combine water, nectar, tequila, sugar, lime peel and lime juice in **CROCK-POT®** Express Crock Multi-Cooker. Place rack in pot. Place pears on rack. Secure lid. Press STEAM, set pressure to HIGH and time to 3 minutes. Make sure Steam Release Valve is in the "Seal" (closed) position. Press START/STOP.

2 Once cooking is complete, quick release pressure. Remove to serving plates and serve warm with poaching liquid.

TEQUILA-POACHED PEARS (SLOW COOK)

MAKES 4 SERVINGS

2 cups water

1 can (11½ ounces) pear nectar

1 cup tequila

½ cup sugar

Grated peel and juice of 1 lime

4 Anjou pears, peeled

1 Combine water, nectar, tequila, sugar, lime peel and lime juice in **CROCK-POT®** Express Crock Multi-Cooker. Place rack in pot. Place pears on rack. Secure lid. Press SLOW COOK, set temperature and time to LOW 4 to 6 hours or to HIGH 2 to 3 hours. Make sure Steam Release Valve is in the "Release" (open) position. Press START/STOP.

2 Once cooking is complete, remove to serving plates and serve warm with poaching liquid.

TIP: Poaching fruit in a sugar, juice or alcohol syrup helps the fruit retain its shape and become more flavorful.

INDEX

METRIC CONVERSION CHART

VOLUME MEASUREMENTS (dry)

$\frac{1}{8}$ teaspoon = 0.5 mL
$\frac{1}{4}$ teaspoon = 1 mL
$\frac{1}{2}$ teaspoon = 2 mL
$\frac{3}{4}$ teaspoon = 4 mL
1 teaspoon = 5 mL
1 tablespoon = 15 mL
2 tablespoons = 30 mL
$\frac{1}{4}$ cup = 60 mL
$\frac{1}{3}$ cup = 75 mL
$\frac{1}{2}$ cup = 125 mL
$\frac{2}{3}$ cup = 150 mL
$\frac{3}{4}$ cup = 175 mL
1 cup = 250 mL
2 cups = 1 pint = 500 mL
3 cups = 750 mL
4 cups = 1 quart = 1 L

VOLUME MEASUREMENTS (fluid)

1 fluid ounce (2 tablespoons) = 30 mL
4 fluid ounces ($\frac{1}{2}$ cup) = 125 mL
8 fluid ounces (1 cup) = 250 mL
12 fluid ounces (1$\frac{1}{2}$ cups) = 375 mL
16 fluid ounces (2 cups) = 500 mL

WEIGHTS (mass)

$\frac{1}{2}$ ounce = 15 g
1 ounce = 30 g
3 ounces = 90 g
4 ounces = 120 g
8 ounces = 225 g
10 ounces = 285 g
12 ounces = 360 g
16 ounces = 1 pound = 450 g

DIMENSIONS

$\frac{1}{16}$ inch = 2 mm
$\frac{1}{8}$ inch = 3 mm
$\frac{1}{4}$ inch = 6 mm
$\frac{1}{2}$ inch = 1.5 cm
$\frac{3}{4}$ inch = 2 cm
1 inch = 2.5 cm

OVEN TEMPERATURES

250°F = 120°C
275°F = 140°C
300°F = 150°C
325°F = 160°C
350°F = 180°C
375°F = 190°C
400°F = 200°C
425°F = 220°C
450°F = 230°C

BAKING PAN SIZES

Utensil	Size in Inches/Quarts	Metric Volume	Size in Centimeters
Baking or	8×8×2	2 L	20×20×5
Cake Pan	9×9×2	2.5 L	23×23×5
(square or	12×8×2	3 L	30×20×5
rectangular)	13×9×2	3.5 L	33×23×5
Loaf Pan	8×4×3	1.5 L	20×10×7
	9×5×3	2 L	23×13×7
Round Layer	8×1½	1.2 L	20×4
Cake Pan	9×1½	1.5 L	23×4
Pie Plate	8×1¼	750 mL	20×3
	9×1¼	1 L	23×3
Baking Dish	1 quart	1 L	—
or Casserole	1½ quart	1.5 L	—
	2 quart	2 L	—